CRACKING
THE
PERSONALITY
CODE

D1501903

Book cover design by:
Lighthouse Publishing Services

Illustration by:
@Barton Stabler/Images.com

ISBN: 1-4392-1233-3
ISBN-13: 9781439212332

Visit www.booksurge.com to order additional copies.

CRACKING

THE

PERSONALITY

CODE

By Dana Borowka, MA *&* Ellen Borowka, MA

www.crackingthepersonalitycode.com
www.lighthouseconsulting.com

⁄⁄⁄ Table of Contents

⫻ Acknowledgements

O NE OF THE greatest things to have come out of writing this book is connecting with Henry DeVries, our collaborator and friend.

Special thanks go out to Birdie; Carol Borowka; Nancy, Glenn and Bentley Croix; Erin and James Croix; Len Jett; Roberta, David, Kiana and Sophia Lee-Smale; Mary and Ted Weeks; and Brian Whittington and Jason Whittington. We also owe a debt of gratitude to Eva and Victor Avalos and family; Jessie Eckhardt and family; Patty Kamson and family; Loretta Banks and family; Pam MacCallum and family; and Sue Stonehouse and family. We would also like to especially thank Dr. Rick Brinkman, Shel Brucker, Dr. Jay Carter, Larry Cassidy, Martha and Barry Deutsch, Vicki and James Elliott and family, Suzanne and Dwight Frindt, Bruce Heller, Rob Hupp, Dr. Rick Kirschner, Dan Kravitz, Lou Kravitz, Susan and Paul LaCombe, Pete Lakey, David Lee, Ann Olson, Rafael Pastor, Boaz Rauchwerger, Brad Remillard, Paul Spiegelman, Mark Terman, Ken Ude and Larry Wilson. This book is also in loving memory of Harry Borowka, Elizabeth Piggot (Aunt Bubba), Margaret St. Claire (Granny), Gerry Bos, Jack Bruce, Mary Lou Crockett and David Tratner.

Last, but not least, we wish to thank: all of our clients and friends, all Vistage International chairs and members who have helped guide us along our journey, Beth Adkisson, Madeleine Albright, Gordon Basichis, Michael Blackwell, David Brecher, Bruce Brier, Barbara Bry, Jim Canfield, Richard Carr, Carole and Dave Carter, Hayden Claisse, Larry Comp, Jeannine Coronado, Ed Cox, Bob Dabic, Tom Drucker, Mary Baker Eddy, Stephen Elson, Lara Fields, Bob Fiest, Moises Figueroa, Thomas Friedman, Richard Galvan, Jim Gerwien, Yolanda Guibert, Linda Harris, Bill Hawfield, Tom Hill,

Ron Hoeffer, Karen Jorgensen, Ken Keller, Eddie Keyes, Joann Klonowski, Mark Lefko, Jim Lehrer, Gary Lockwood, Celia and Ted Margison, Judy Marshall-Benson, Phil Matthews, John Monroe, Marilyn Murphy, Dana's entire Vistage International Group, Jack Napoli, Nora Paller, Steve Paulin, Mitch Pearlman, Ron Penland, John Perry, Tom Peters, Steve Puente, Scott Rabinowitz, Kevin Rafferty, Susan and Gary Reuben, Sharon Valdez and Don Riddell, Alan Rothenberg, Paul Ruseabagina, Gary Saenger, Dan Savage, Jim Tenuto, Monica Urquidi, Elena Vasquez, Patty Vogan, Joe Vona Jr., Joe Vona Sr., Paul David Walker, Greg Wells, Teresa and Les Whitney, Ward Wieman, George Will, Mikki Williams, Henry Wong, Bob Woodward and Steve Zuback.

⅏ Praise for This Book

As authors Dana and Ellen Borowka bring to light, more than half of all new hires fail at the job. That means their employers are not just shorting themselves, but also their customers, business partners, and shareholders who also absorb the mistakes and mishaps from these poor choices. *Cracking the Personality Code* analyzes why so many managers get it wrong and then provides the diagnostics to help businesses recruit and retain top-notch talent. By following the Borowkas' learnings, leaders like those within our Vistage International community of senior-level executives will not only save time, money, and energy, they may also save face among their peers and other constituents.

— Rafael Pastor, Chairman of the Board and CEO, Vistage International

Dana and Ellen Borowka have cracked the code. They provide inspiration, wisdom and tools for hiring and managing any team. This is a book you will refer to again and again.

— Larry Wilson, author of *Play to Win*

For the past fifteen years, Dana and Ellen have been instrumental in helping me to understand people and build effective teams. Their testing and expertise in analyzing the data have clearly increased our batting average in hiring the "right" person for the job and in building and motivating effective teams. I was thrilled to hear that they were writing a book to introduce their techniques to others. It's all about putting the right people in the right positions and building effective teams.

— Ken Ude, President/CEO, Stila Cosmetics

Placing the right people in the right position calls for strategic and long-term planning in our multinational family business. My experience proves that work style and personality assessments help speed up the mutual understanding and effective communication among family members and staff. *"Cracking The Personality Code"* is able to share with us how greater insight in personality increases team building to meet the challenges we face in the global economy.

— David Lee, Director, Lee Kum Kee Co. Ltd. Chairman, Family Learning & Development Center & Family Foundation

I am thrilled that Dana and Ellen have finally written a book to share what I have known for years by working with them—that the power of personality testing serves companies not only to determine whom to hire, but how to work together to build a cohesive team. Running a successful business is about managing people, and this great work will help you manage the personalities of those who will get you from here to there.

— Paul Spiegelman, CEO, The Beryl Companies

Hiring isn't easy...people put forth what they want you to see and hear. The process that is shared in *Cracking the Personality Code* is based on a scientific approach to avoid hiring and managing by chance. Advertising Sales is one of the most competitive industries in the US. Dana and Ellen have been responsible for us having one of the best retention rates in our industry.

— James G. Elliott, President, The James G. Elliott Company

⫻ Foreword

Jack was in his late thirties. He had worked for large companies for fifteen years and finally decided to take what he knew and start his own business. He ran the numbers, talked to friends and advisors, and determined that with hard work he could get by in the first year, and from the second year on, do very well.

It was the "hard work" that was the problem. Not the actual work: Jack worked 12–14 hour days. The problem was that Jack only had so many hours in a day. He could not get all the work done. So he decided to hire an office assistant to take tasks off his back and free up time to go after the big bucks.

And then Jack hired a few production employees. Then a shop manager. Next a sales person. Then a bookkeeper, and of course, an office manager. As year #2 rolled on, Jack looked up and he had a—a—a company. A real company, with real people. Eight employees, soon ten, not long until twenty or even thirty.

The more employees, the more variety. Of course. Jack wanted different skills to match up with the different challenges faced by the firm. The problem to which Jack awoke at the dawn of year #3 was two-fold: employees who varied from what he wanted in terms of skills and capability; and employees who just didn't "fit in" (get along with, work well with, or act as team players) with the other employees.

How could Jack have avoided this uneven performance or behavioral mismatch? How do you avoid the same issues? Actually, there is no way to get it right all of the time. These are *people* we are hiring and with whom we are dealing. However, we can narrow the gap between what we want and what we get, often by a considerable amount. We can do this by a series of thoughtful steps that lead up to the actual hiring:

1. Define the values and environment that you wish to promote in your firm.

2. Define the position for which you are hiring, including core skills and related behaviors required for success in the position.

3. Utilize a capable mechanism to identify and source qualified candidates.

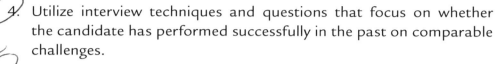

4. Utilize interview techniques and questions that focus on whether the candidate has performed successfully in the past on comparable challenges.

5. And—utilize a valid testing instrument to assist in determining appropriate interview questions and to define possible issues to be explored with the candidate.

In the main, this book deals with assessing the candidate and his/her "fit" and, as part of the process, utilizing an evaluative instrument. In other words, Step 5 above. There are several of testing instruments available. Most have value and can provide direction and/or insights you would not experience without such an organized look at the candidate.

The book will talk about the details related to using a testing instrument in hiring. In creating a lead-in for this discussion, my observations are as follows:

➤ Other than "socializing" reasons (i.e., we tend to like to work with and around other people), we hire others to extend our work footprint. That is code for: we hire others to do work we do not want to do, or do not have time to do, or cannot do as well as the person we hire.

➤ We pay the person we hire "out of our pocket." In other words, what the business makes is now split between you and whomever you hire. So if you are going to hand over part of the loot, you had better be getting something very good in return.

➤ A good place to start is that the person hired creates more additional loot than you pay the person. The greater the excess, the greater your return on hiring the person (if you buy a machine, you expect a return; why is spending comparable dollars on an employee any different?).

➤ Thus, doing the very best job possible of assessing the candidate is important (even crucial). Can he/she do enough more, or do something better by enough, to create revenue adequate to cover his/her cost plus create an attractive return?

If it were my dollars in play, I would use all types of useful tools in making this assessment. That includes a quality-testing instrument.

I would pick carefully the instrument and, every bit as important, the person administering the instrument and assessing the results. I would discuss with the administrator all aspects of the position and related behaviors.

Finally, I would understand that any instrument is just one input to the hiring process and decision (along with the resume, interviews, discussion among interviewers, references, etc.). The results are to be respected, but not to be held as determinant.

I welcome you to the following pages and to the opportunity to explore using quality testing instruments to improve your hiring results, along with your bottom line.

— **Larry Cassidy**
  Vistage International Chair

Larry Cassidy, the chair of five Vistage International groups in Orange County, California, was the first in the company's fifty-year history to facilitate 1,000 Vistage International meetings. Vistage International (formerly known as TEC) is a CEO peer group organization that focuses on executive performance. Cassidy, a former CEO himself, has been involved with Vistage International since 1986 and has counseled 300 business leaders. Cassidy has been recognized with numerous awards including Vistage International's highest honor, the Don Cope Memorial Award, presented annually to the top Vistage International Chair.

Part One

The Challenge

1

⁄⁄⁄ A Code Worth Cracking

You Never Know Until It Is Too Late

AS THE OLD saying goes, "You never know someone until you work with them, travel with them, or live with them."

Naturally, all managers want to select the right people. Alas, it doesn't always work out that way.

Without a doubt, the toughest challenge for a manager is consistently hiring quality people. However, many managers feel hiring is no better than the flip of a coin because roughly fifty percent of all newly hired people fail to meet expectations.

Typically managers are frustrated by a lack of improved results, despite their best efforts to improve interviewing techniques, background screening, and resume checks. No matter what they seem to do, nothing improves the odds.

Of course, managers know the stakes are high. As management visionary Peter Drucker said, "Of all the decisions an executive makes, none are as important as the decisions about people because they ultimately determine the performance capacity of the organization" (Drucker, 1986, *The Frontiers of Management*).

Hiring the wrong people results in reduced time to market, a loss of market share, money and time wasted on training, higher turnover rates among productive sales people, lost management time, increased stress from people problems, lost customers to the competition, and the tremendous opportunity cost of unmet sales goals.

But don't lose hope, because there is good news. Behavioral research has proven there is a better way to make hiring decisions. According to a study of 20,000 new hires, 46% failed within the first eighteen months (*IndustryWeek*, October 5, 2005). The more telling statistic was why they failed: only 11% because they lacked necessary technical skills—81% were for behavioral reasons. The study of 5,247 hiring managers found that 26% of new hires fail because they can't accept feedback, 23% because they are unable to understand and manage emotions, 17% because they lack the necessary motivation to excel, and 15% because they have the wrong temperament for the job.

Yet, although many managers find personality profiling assessments like Myers-Briggs or DISC to be interesting, they don't see how they would be of real value in the hiring process. (No wonder, because these are the wrong tools for the job, like trying to pound a nail with a screwdriver or cut a board with a hammer).

These managers are resigned to the belief that nothing can be done to improve hiring results. They cite research like the massive study conducted by the University of Michigan on the futility of accurately predicting later success on the job. The surprise finding was that the typical interview only increases the likelihood of choosing the best candidate by less than 2%. In other words, if you just tossed a coin you would be correct 50% of the time. If you added an interview you would only be right 52% of the time. (John & Rhonda Hunter, July 1984, "Validity and Utility of Alternative Predictors of Job Performance," *Psychological Bulletin*).

While getting the best candidate is the goal, often you get stuck with a real loser. The Corporate Leadership Council, an association of human resources executives, found that 40% of new hires need to be dismissed within the first year and a half—others will just hang on, treading water (*Entrepreneur Magazine*, Feb. 2005).

Because of these and other similar studies, many managers accept the high new hire failure rates as a cost of doing business. They believe hiring is just a numbers game and everyone gets stuck with their share of clunkers.

But this is a miscalculated view. There exists an expanding body of knowledge that some have discovered improve their hiring practices. A McKinsey & Company study of 13,000 executives at 120 companies found that the top one-fifth of companies that do the best job of attracting and attaining top talent earned, on average, 22 percentage points higher return to shareholders than industry peers (Michaels, Handfield-Jones and Axelrod, 2000, *The War for Talent*).

To improve hiring decisions, many companies have found out how to crack the personality code by using robust personality testing. Personality tests are a standard recruiting practice for many branches of the government and military, as well as many Fortune 500 companies when assessing potential hires for key or critical positions. This is not guesswork or an untested science.

Why do roughly 30% of all companies, including big names like Wal-Mart and General Motors, subject their applicants and employees to some sort of personality test?

Think of all the lost opportunities and hidden costs associated with bad hiring and bad managing. The total financial impact can include reduced time to market, lost revenue from incomplete projects, and failed execution of strategies. This results in untold lost profits and productivity.

While reasonable experts may disagree about specific salary-to-cost ratios, the fact remains that the cost of new employee failure is much higher than merely search costs and salary. Those are just two of the direct costs.

Indirect costs typically add up to much more.

Some of the direct and indirect costs noted in various studies we reviewed include:

> wasted salary, benefits, and severance.
> higher turnover rates among productive employees.
> damage to reputation and market share.
> lost management time.
> increased stress and anxiety from people problems.
> lost recruitment fees and training costs.
> lower personal productivity among dissatisfied employees.
> disruptions caused by dissatisfied employees.

"Multiplied across ten million businesses in North America, it is obvious that bad hires cost billions of dollars every year," says Barry Deutsch, a principal of the executive recruiting firm, Impact Hiring Solutions.

"Sadly, this is a game in which everyone loses. The person hurt most just might be the executive who was set up for failure. This person accepted a position based on a vague job description, and then found reality did not match up to their perceptions." adds Deutsch.

⚜ *The Cost of One Bad Hire: A Worksheet*

To help you get a more concrete idea of the costs of a bad hire, here is a worksheet compiled by Impact Hiring Solutions. Deutsch advises hiring managers to take the time to fill it out as completely as possible. Even if you guesstimate at times, you'll find the bottom line enlightening—and probably alarming. (For more insights on how to hire smarter, see Deutsch's advice in Chapter 4.)

Direct Costs		
Hiring Costs	**Calculate for entire search, all candidates**	
	Recruiting fees	$
	Assessment/background check fees	$
	Employee referral incentives/fees	$
	HR department time and expenses	$
	Executive/department interviewer time and expenses	$
	Travel expenses (candidates, families, HR, recruiters)	$
	Total Hiring Costs	**$**
Compensation	**Calculate for duration of employment**	
	Salary	$
	Bonuses	$
	Benefits	$
	Relocation costs	$
	"Perks" (autos, club memberships, etc.)	$
	Paid time off/vacation/sick pay	$
	Stock options	$
	Total Compensation Costs	$
Severance	Severance pay	$
	Legal costs	$
	Outplacement or retraining costs	$
	HR and other staff time/expenses related to termination	$
	Total Severance Costs	**$**
	Total Direct Costs	**$**

Indirect Costs		
Support Costs	Support personnel time and expenses (i.e., executive assistants)	$
	Office space, equipment, network resources, training	$
	Expenses, mileage, travel costs	$
Cost of Poor Performance	Poor execution (failed product launches, missed earnings targets, poor reputation due to missed on-time-deliveries/quality, etc.)	$
	Missed opportunities (losing business to competitors, being second in product launches, missed opportunities to enter new markets, etc.)	$
	Lawsuits (include legal representation costs, judgments, executive and board time, and expenses)	$
Cost of Poor Subordinate/ Department Morale	"Trickle-down" cost of poor performance among subordinates, departments, and divisions (estimate if necessary)	$
	Turnover among subordinates due to poor morale, mismanagement (include costs of hiring replacements)	$
	Total Indirect Costs	**$**

Most hiring managers are often astounded when they see, in black and white, how much it really costs to hire the wrong person.

❧ *Why and How to Use Personality Testing*

WHILE WE ARE staunch advocates of personality testing, we admit there are limits to its power. If you meet a profiling organization that says you can decide to hire or not hire based on test data alone, please walk away. No, run away. Personality testing is not a silver bullet or magic potion.

The secret is to cultivate top performers through a three-step process: assess candidates with personality profiling, screen candidates for behavioral tendencies, and manage more effectively based on behavioral styles. The goal is to base your hiring and managing decisions on the best data that can be collected.

No matter how good an interviewer you are, you are not getting the full picture during an interview. The next step has to do with background and reference checks and personality assessments. What criteria should you use to screen personality tests? Here are some questions you need to ask:

> ➢ What training or degrees are required for interpretation of the data? Tests that only require a weekend training program to interpret data can be problematic since testing is a very complex subject. When making hiring or internal decisions, managers need as much information and understanding as possible because the consequences can be costly.

> ➢ If you hire a testing company, do they also review the person's resume? We suggest you make sure that the testing company requires that they are provided with the resume as part of the process so it is used when reviewing the assessment.

> ➢ Does the test you use have a scale for "impression management" to understand the accuracy of results and determine if the test taker is trying to "fake good?" The questionnaire needs a minimum of 164 questions to gather enough data for this scale.

> ➢ How many clinical studies conducted by major universities have there been to validate the test? There should be multiple studies for validation purposes.

> ➢ What is the history of the profile? You should know where the test came from and how long it has been in use.

> ➤ How often is the normative database updated and where is the data coming from? For instance, it might be drawn from the 1990 or 2000 U.S. Census.

> ➤ Is a cultural bias built in to the profile and for what countries?

> ➤ Does the profile meet U.S. government employment standards, and has it been reviewed for ADA compliance?

> ➤ Does the test examine career matching? You need to ask how many careers and occupations have been studied and is the database validated by outside organizations or only by in-house studies. What is most important is if the individual has a similar thought pattern that meets the criteria within the job description.

> ➤ What reading level is required? For instance, it might be for a ninth grade or a fifth grade English level.

> ➤ What is the number of profiles that have been administered?

> ➤ What is the number of actual primary "Big Five" scales used? Many tests will claim to have more scales than they actually have.

> ➤ Does the testing company give off any common warning signs? For instance, when a testing company representative uses absolute statements when describing human behavior, like "people are all the same" or "people don't change." Or when someone claims their test is 98 or 99 percent accurate, a claim which rarely can be clinically supported. (If you hear this, think long and hard before doing business with this company.)

> ➤ Does the data provide the depth necessary to understand how an individual is wired inside? If they only use four primary scales, that is not sufficient.

> ➤ What are the validity, reliability, and basis of the test?

These are some general questions. If a profile falls short in any area, we strongly suggest additional research into the accuracy of the data being generated. This book will give you what the best answers should be to all these questions.

While personality testing can be a valuable resource before you hire, perhaps the true value of any assessment comes in using the insights it provides along the entire spectrum of employment. Personality assessments lend objectivity to decisions that may otherwise be largely subjective.

A proper test should reach beyond simple profiles and decipher an employee's underlying needs. This is key for employee development, team building, conflict resolution, and succession planning.

Below are nine ways to use personality testing in the workplace to help bring out the best in your employees at all levels in an organization.

1. Get the real picture. Of course every candidate wants to put their best foot forward during an interview. However, through a personality test, you uncover a great deal about their ability to work well with other personalities, their problem-solving abilities, their thought processes, and their ability to tolerate stress. Personality testing gives you objective information that can help you make an informed decision about if this person is a good fit for the job and for the team. If you decided to hire the person, the questions you ask during the hiring process will reduce your learning curve as a manager on how best to manage this person from day one.

2. Help them be all that they can be. Everyone has strengths and weaknesses. Find out the real truth with an objective measure. Once you pinpoint the good and the bad, you can place them in the right position and coach them on where to improve.

3. Take me to your leaders. Personality testing gives the manager and employees a common language about how they like to interact. The assessments can help you train future managers on how to get the best out of the team.

4. Know how to manage difficult people. Face it, there will always be difficult people and flare ups on the job. Use objective personality assessments to diagnose potential sources of workplace conflict. The best way to deal with a problem is to prevent it in the first place.

5. Get everybody to play nice. Sales and marketing, operations and financial people have to interact to make the company run smoothly. Too many employees get frustrated with other co-workers and just wonder why everyone doesn't act like them. Through the use of personality profiles managers can coach employees how to interact better with peers.

6. Treat co-workers the way they want to be treated. In today's fast-paced world of business there is little time to get to know many of your co-workers. Using personality assessments as the basis for team building exercises can quickly get everyone to have a healthier respect for other ways of seeing the world.

7. Make managers better leaders. The days of seat-of-the-pants leadership are over. When managers understand what makes their people tick, they can be better leaders. Knowing personality traits can help with motivating teams, communicating change, and delegating authority.

8. Pick better teams. Today, much work is done by ad-hoc teams that come together for a specific purpose. Before you assemble a team it pays to know the strengths and weaknesses of the team members. Sometimes this can be the difference between a productive team that gets the job done and one that pulls apart at the seams.

9. Set employees up for success. Sometimes we hire the right employee and put them in the wrong job. Understanding preferred work styles and where a person would be happiest goes a long way to improving retention and productivity.

⫸ *What's Ahead*

THIS BOOK EXPLAINS the essentials of what managers and business owners need to know about hiring and managing employees with the help of personality testing. We believe the personality code can be cracked. If that sounds like a bold declaration, consider this: Studies show that personality tests are a far more reliable predictor of performance than interviews and resumes.

As a manager responsible for hiring and managing employees, this book will provide you with the basics of using personality tests in hiring and managing.

Chapter 2 is about choosing the personality test that is right for you. Not all tests are created equal. In fact, some are wrong for the task and others are just plain illegal.

In Chapter 3, we look at the science behind the profiling tools. While much of the work was done in the time period between World War I and II, some of the universal truths go back to the Greek era of Socrates and Plato. We also look at historic decisions in the legal world to examine what you can and can't do when it comes to testing. You have heard the adage that ignorance of the law is no excuse? Ignorance of personality testing law is just plain bad business.

Chapter 4 provides insights on how to improve the entire hiring and candidate screening process. For this chapter we are indebted to the insights of our good friends Barry Deutsch and Brad Remillard of Impact Hiring Solutions, authors of the book, *You're Not the Person I Hired*.

Our proprietary process for testing candidates and employees that you manage is the subject of Chapter 5. To eliminate a manager's natural tendency to focus on the likeability of the person, we developed a structured tool to help you objectively and comprehensively evaluate personality. The Personics Factor Matrix™ is the tool we have our clients use to gain insight into personality of a candidate during the hiring process.

Chapter 6 examines how to manage employees better by understanding the personality traits of those who report to you. If you want to be better understood by your employees, first take the time to understand what makes them tick.

Chapter 7 deals with that challenging time when you need to get an employee off your team. The hope is to help the employee transition to a better career move. In that excellent business book *Good to Great*, Jim Collins uses the metaphor of making sure you have the right people on your bus. This chapter is about getting people off your bus—and in a humane fashion.

Perhaps the most important topic of all—how to deal with difficult people—is the focus of Chapter 8. Nothing can poison a workplace like a difficult employee. There is an art and science of dealing with these people.

In Chapter 9, now that you have cracked the personality code, what's next? Suzanne and Dwight Frindt, founders of the leadership-development firm 2130 Partners, explain how to become a vision-focused leader around whom issues can be raised and resolved productively.

In Chapter 10, we have some parting thoughts on cracking the interpersonal communication code through insight and empathy.

Finally, we wrap up by giving a list of books to obtain as you continue to master cracking the personality code. School is never out for the professional. With so much to choose from to read and so little time to do it, as a closing gift for our time together we wanted to offer our recommendations on where to go from here.

While this book will help improve your hiring process and your ability to effectively manage employees, the information here is of a general nature and not intended as legal advice nor a substitute for getting specific legal advice on your particular situation. With that caution in mind, let's turn to the process for cracking the personality code.

2

☲ Choosing Your Test

Ranking Profiling Tools

NOT TO ALARM you, but don't take choosing a personality test lightly. Did you know your organization risks lawsuits if it fails to do proper due diligence in test selection? That's because there are a multitude of assessments available out there, and the industry is totally unregulated.

Today there are around 2,500 cognitive and personality tests on the market. So how do you decide which one to use? To understand how to choose from the plethora of personality tests, it is helpful to understand the origins of these instruments.

Our story begins in a mental hospital in Minnesota during World War II. A test called the Minnesota Multiphasic Personality Inventory is created to diagnose mental illness with yes-or-no responses to a series of questions. In an attempt to put some science into the hiring process, many companies started to employ psychologists, who in turn used this existing MMPI psychopathological test to screen job applicants. The test included true-false questions like "I never indulge in unusual sex practices" and "I feel sure there is only one true religion." Of course, this seemed strange and intrusive to most job applicants who took the test over the next six decades.

Meanwhile, a Harvard University instructor and psychologist named Raymond Cattell was working in the Adjutant General's office devises psychological tests for the military. After the war, he accepted a research professorship at the University of Illinois where they developed the first electronic computer, the Illiac I that will make it possible for the first time to do large-scale factor analyses of his personality testing theories.

Cattell used an IBM sorter and the brand-new Illiac computer to perform factor analysis on 4,500 personality-related words. The result was a test to measure intelligence and to assess personality traits known as the Sixteen Personality Factor questionnaire (16PF). First published in 1949, the 16PF profiles individuals using sixteen different personality traits. Cattell's research proved that while most people have surface personality traits that can be easily observed, we also have source traits that can be discovered only by the statistical processes of factor analysis. His sixteen measures of personality are:

> - Warmth—from reserved to attentive
> - Reasoning—from concrete thinker to conceptual thinker
> - Emotional Stability—from changeable to stable
> - Dominance—from cooperative to assertive
> - Liveliness—from restrained to spontaneous
> - Rule Consciousness—from non-conforming to dutiful
> - Social Boldness—from timid to bold
> - Sensitivity—from unsentimental to sentimental
> - Vigilance—from trusting to suspicious
> - Abstractedness—from practical to imaginative
> - Privateness—from openness to discreet
> - Apprehension—from self-assured to apprehensive
> - Openness to Change—from traditional to open to change
> - Self-Reliance—from affiliative to individualistic
> - Perfectionism—from tolerant of disorder to perfectionistic
> - Tension—from relaxed to tense

In 1963, W.T. Norman verified Cattell's work but felt that only five factors shape personality: extraversion, independence, self-control, anxiety, and tough-mindedness. Dubbed the "Big Five" approach, this has become the basis of many of the modern personality tests on the market today. There have been hundreds and hundreds of studies validating the approach.

Using the "Big Five" terms, here is what a manager is looking for on a spectrum of personality:

- Extraversion—introvert or extravert?
- Independence—accommodation or independence?
- Self-Control—lack of restraint or self-control?
- Anxiety—low anxiety or high anxiety?
- Tough-Mindedness—receptivity or resolute?

The five decades of research findings, which are much more elaborate then the brief descriptions provided here, have served as the framework for constructing a number of derivative personality inventories. For comparison, this table shows the different terms used for the Big Five factors.

Authors	Test	1	2	3	4	5
Cattell	16 PF	Extraversion	Independence	Self-Control	Anxiety	Tough-Mindedness
Jackson	PRF	Extraversion	Agreeableness	Achievement/Methodicalness	Independence	Openness
Costa & McRae	NEO-PI-R	Extraversion	Agreeableness	Conscientiousness	Neuroticism	Openness
Hogan & Hogan	HPI	Ambition/Sociability	Likeability	Prudence	Adjustment	Intellect/school success
Goldberg	IPIP	Surgency	Agreeableness	Conscientiousness	Emotional Stability	Intellect

"This is a topic that's been researched to death by the field of industrial and organizational psychology," said Peter Cappelli, Management Professor and Director of the Center for Human Resources at the Wharton School of the University of Pennsylvania, to *Inc.* magazine in August 2006. "The amazing thing is how few companies take this seriously. It's kind of mind-boggling that they would undertake such huge investments and not pay attention to what we know about how to pick out the people who are going to be the best."

◆ *Ranking Personality Tests*

WHAT CRITERIA SHOULD you use to screen hiring tests and assessment companies? Naturally you want to know how long the profile has been around and what is the history. You should know how many people have used the test and in how many companies. Then you should dig deeper. Here is what we look for:

> How much training or degrees are required to interpret the results? (Data interpretation is the most important factor when reviewing results.)

> Are enough scales used to cover the human personality? (A minimum of twelve primary scales is needed for new hire assessments to get a complete picture. Both DISC and Myers-Briggs only have four primary scales and do not collect enough data to give a full picture.)

> Is the test properly validated and on what basis?

> Is the test reliable and on what basis?

> Is the test legal, and has it been reviewed for ADA compliance and gender, culture, and racial bias?

> Would the test leave a negative impression with job candidates?

> Is it proper for both hiring and managing?

> What reading level is required to take the test?

To help you screen personality tests and testing companies, we have compiled the following nine-point checklist you can use to review assessment tools and support.

1. Qualifications of the individual who is interpreting the test. In addition, we also believe the best tests require someone with comprehensive psychological training or degrees for proper interpretation of the data. Weekend training programs can be problematic since testing and human behavior is a very complex subject. When making hiring or internal decisions, organizations need as much information and understanding as possible as the consequences can be very costly.

2. **Number of personality scales.** The assessment company providing the test needs to address the number of scales they are using. A primary scale represents a personality trait. The more scales, the clearer the picture of the individual's personality. Scales are similar to pixels on a screen—the more pixels the better the picture. When making hiring or personnel decisions, it is better to have as clear and accurate a picture as possible. That is why we suggest having a minimum of twelve primary scales. Many profiles tend to use a bipolar or spectrum scale format. An example of a spectrum scale would have "Dominance" at one end of the scale with "Cooperative" at the other end so that the scale score defines how dominant or cooperative the individual is. This would be considered one scale. However, some organizations might try to count a spectrum scale on their profile as two scales rather than one. This is a *very* important point since some organizations will actually state their profiles have double the scales than what is reality and would misrepresent their profile. It is best to always ask the testing organization how many primary and subscales the profile has. The number of scales does not determine the length of time it takes to take the profile. Some 12-scale profiles can take up to an hour and a half while a 16-scale profile can take 35 to 45 minutes to complete.

Using twelve or more scales is the most cost effective because the personality assessments can be used for both screening candidates and for team building. We feel this offers the best return on investment for a manager because they can first have their existing team of employees tested, and then use the data to best judge how new hires will work with the existing team.

3. **Impression management/"faking good" scale.** A questionnaire needs a minimum of 164 questions to gather enough data for an "impression management" scale. Impression management allows you to understand the accuracy of the results and if someone is trying to "fake good." When someone scores high on the impression management scale, it means they chose more socially desirable answers to the profile questions. This type of response may be based on self-deception or deception of others where the individual then has a need to manage their impression on others. *This is a very complex subject and is a vital scale to have in a profile. Otherwise, you don't know if the profile data is accurate. Regarding this topic, we would highly recommend discussing it in more depth with an expert in the field of profile interpretation.*

4. Link profile to resume and job description. It is not enough to just review the data analysis of a potential new hire's personality. Before you hire this person, you will want to ascertain how the person's past relates to the possible future your position offers. Whoever is assessing the data of the candidate with the hiring manager needs to have the resume and the job description in order to do a thorough job of reviewing the data. A proper test analyzes personality characteristics in the context of business concerns:

> Coping with stress
> Interpersonal and social skills
> Problem solving
> Organizational role patterns
> Ability to get along with others
> Potential weaknesses

5. Amount of time it takes to take the test. How long should it take to complete a test? That depends on how in-depth you need to look at personality. Here are your typical three options for testing:

> Basic team assessments using four primary scales with 30–60 questions can take 10–20 minutes to complete.
> Simple prescreening of candidates/team assessments using up to eight scales with 60–120 questions can take 20–30 minutes to complete.
> In-depth personality tests for screening candidates and assessing the team using 12–16 scales with more than 164 questions can take 35–90 minutes to complete.

6. Thought flow. Of course, not everyone thinks and processes information the same way. A good personality test will give you insight into an individual's thought flow. This not only helps with hiring, but understanding how someone's thoughts naturally flow is also a very powerful management tool. Sharing this information amongst the team helps employees communicate more effectively with other members of the team.

7. Career matching. Certain personality tests help you gain information which may either support the person's present career choices or assist them to explore, consider, and plan for another career direction.

A personality test can give you an indication of which jobs match the candidate's personality type and for which careers they may have an aptitude. You do need to remember that the test results are only an indicator and should not be relied on as an absolute assessment of which career is best for the person.

8. Strengths and weaknesses summary. Personality testing is a proven and effective way to create highly functional teams. This starts with a summary of each person's strengths and weaknesses. Once you know which personality types work best together, you can mix and match your people so that you get the most out of each of them. For every strength a person possesses there is a corresponding weakness. Being assertive is a strength. However, a person can be too assertive and off-putting for some people or in some situations.

9. Detailed interview questions. The assessment company you choose should help you create tailored interview questions based on the candidate's specific personality. The purpose is to probe facets of the personality on which you need more details. Many employers are now doing "behavioral interviews." Rather than focusing on resume and accomplishments alone, use the personality test as a jumping off point to ask open-ended questions that will cause the job candidate to describe real circumstances and their responses to them. Ask them to describe in detail a particular event, project, or experience, how they dealt with the situation, and what the outcome was. This type of interviewing is the most accurate predictor of future performance.

Part Two

 **Hiring**

3

⁄⁄⁄ The Science behind Profiles

Scientific Breakthroughs and Historic Legal Decisions

DID YOU KNOW that the term personality is derived from the Greek word *persona*, or mask, associated with the dramatic masks worn by actors in ancient Greek comedies and tragedies? The irony today is that personality testing is designed to uncover the true personality a job candidate or employee may be masking.

The following is a historic timeline of personality types, including the scientific breakthroughs of the last century. Events are covered from the ancient Chinese and Greeks to the giants of the early 1900s like Carl Jung and Raymond Cattell. We conclude with a few legal words to the wise about personality testing.

2200 BCE
Nothing is new under the sun. As early as 2200 BCE the Chinese used oral examinations to hire and retain civil servants.

2000 BCE
Personality types are part of the earliest known writings. Both the Epic of Gilgamesh and the Bible contain passages indicating an awareness that people have different personalities.

460 BCE

In ancient Greece, the physician Hippocrates (460–377 BCE) systematically described the four temperaments of people as "humors" (moods). These were based on the four elements of fire, air, water, and earth and were believed to be responsible for a different type of behavior. Hippocrates recorded the first known personality model, postulating that one's personality is based upon these four moods. Around 340 BCE Plato described the four temperaments as philosopher, guardian, artisan, and scientist.

202 BCE

In China, the Han Dynasty begins testing civil service candidates two centuries before the birth of Jesus Christ. By 1370 CE, the test includes writing essays and poems, a three-day exam, and a final test in Peking now known as Beijing (and you thought your last interview was tough). The system was not abandoned until 1906.

200 CE

Roman physician Claudius Galen (129–216) adopted Hippocrates' method, but it fell out of use in the Middle Ages. Galen expounded upon the theory of four body fluids. He added that different diseases and behaviors have roots in the four humors, which he called temperaments. He identifies them as sanguine, phlegm, cholera, and melancholy. Predominance of blood over other fluids causes a sanguine body. Such a person shall be optimistic, warm, and confident. Predominance of respiratory fluids causes a phlegmatic body. That person shall behave apathetically, sluggishly, and indifferently. Predominance of yellow bile causes a choleric body. That person shall behave angrily, violently, and aggressively. Predominance of black bile causes a melancholic body. Such a person shall fall into depression, sadness, and melancholy.

The Dark Ages

Not much happened on the personality front until the Renaissance.

1798

Perhaps because the famous European philosopher Immanual Kant described the Hippocrates' terms in his 1798 book *Anthropologie*, we still use terms that describe them today: an excess of blood made a person sanguine, too much yellow bile choleric, too much black bile melancholic, and an excess of phlegm of course made one phlegmatic.

1869

Francis Galton argues there are measurable differences between individuals' minds, introducing the idea of psychological testing.

1879

Physiologist Wilhelm Wundt was the first person to separate personality from human body functions. Further, he theorized that temperaments could not simply be limited to the bodily fluids. He believed that no individual was completely of one temperament; rather that everyone typically has varying proportions of two or more. He believed that all four temperaments were basic dimensions of the human personality and that the temperaments fell along the axis of "changeability" and the axis of "emotionality."

1900

In 1900, Sigmund Freud (1859–1939) published *The Interpretation of Dreams* and exerted unprecedented influence on both psychiatric and popular approaches to understanding personality for the next fifty years. The father of psychoanalysis, Freud gave the world such concepts as the ego, free association, and the Oedipus complex. From 1902 to 1912, Freud's two most important colleagues were the Viennese physician, Alfred Adler, and the Swiss psychiatrist, Carl Jung. Adler became famous for such concepts as the inferiority complex and sibling rivalry. Jung devised one of the earliest personality instruments: the word association test ("If I say father, what's the first word that comes to your mind?"). Stay tuned for more about Dr. Jung.

1917

The American Psychological Association asks Robert Woodworth for a test to assess emotional stability. The first modern personality test was the Woodworth Personal data sheet, which was first used in 1919. It was designed to help the United States Army screen out recruits who might be susceptible to shell shock.

1921

The Rorschach inkblot test was introduced in 1921 as a way to determine personality by the interpretation of abstract inkblots.

1921

Carl Jung, the founder of analytical psychology, in his book *Personality Types* was the first to theorize that people always prefer certain identifiable behaviors if they are given a free choice. He also said that on the basis of human preferences, they can be divided in different personality types. Jung's unique and broadly influential approach to psychology has emphasized understanding the psyche through exploring the worlds of dreams, art, mythology, world religion, and philosophy. Although he was a theoretical psychologist and practicing clinician for most of his life, much of his life's work was spent exploring other realms, including Eastern and Western philosophy, alchemy, astrology, sociology, as well as literature and the arts. His most notable contributions include his concept of the psychological archetype, the collective unconscious, and his theory of synchronicity. Some say Jung developed a personality typology that has become so popular that many people don't realize he did anything else. Jung's begins with the distinction between introversion and extroversion. Introverts are people who prefer their internal world of thoughts, feelings, fantasies, dreams, and so on, while extroverts prefer the external world of things, people, and activities.

1923

Today's most popular method (albeit not the best for hiring) is an assessment tool called the Myers-Briggs Type Indicator, which is taken by over four million people annually in over sixteen different languages. The MBTI method was developed over a period of forty years by Isabel Briggs Myers and her mother, Katharine Cook Briggs, and grew from their encounters, in 1923, with the ideas of Carl Jung's psychological types: Sensing, Intuitive, Feeling, and Thinking. Myers further developed Jung's ideas into a system to provide an easy way for everyone to understand and appreciate the Jungian types.

1926

William Moulton Marston, a psychologist at Harvard University, published a book in 1926 describing the DISC system titled *The Emotions of Normal People*. (At that time most behavior work was being done to explain the actions of the criminally insane.) The system first came to prominence as part of the U.S. Army's recruitment process during the years preceding WWII, and then became a popular tool in the commercial sector. The four categories of the DISC human behavior response system are (D) Dominance, (I) Influencing, (S) Steadiness, and (C) Compliance.

1933

Louis Thurstone, in 1933, noted that a list of sixty adjectives on an assessment he developed could be reduced to five meaningful factors. Yet amazingly, little work was done by Thurstone himself or others to follow up and replicate this finding. Allport and Odbert (1936) combed through the English language and found over 4,500 adjectives that are used to describe personality, and formed the primary starting point for Raymond Cattell, renowned psychologist and creator of the 16PF assessment in 1946.

1943

The Thematic Apperception Test was commissioned by the Office of Strategic Services (OSS), precursor to the CIA, in the 1930s to identify personalities that might be susceptible to being turned by enemy intelligence. In 1943, the OSS began putting would-be spies through exercises in a Fairfax, Virginia, countryside home that mimicked on-the-job experiences like interrogating ersatz prisoners of war, creating fake propaganda plans, and recovering secret documents from an enemy agent's room.

1943

The Minnesota Multiphasic Personality Inventory was published in 1943 as a way to aid in assessing psychopathology in a clinical setting. Critics raised issues about the ethics of administering personality tests, especially for non-clinical uses. By the 1960s, tests like the MMPI were being given by companies to employees and applicants as often as to psychiatric patients.

1946

Raymond Cattell did not invent personality testing nor did he invent the computer. He just married the two. Cattell used an IBM sorter and the brand-new Illiac computer to perform factor analysis on 4,500 personality-related words at the University of Illinois. His Sixteen Personality Factors (16PF) test was developed in 1946 and has remained the gold standard in the business world since it was first published in 1949. As the name implies, Cattell found sixteen personality factors that accounted for the majority of trait terms used to describe personality. Through factor analysis, Cattell identified what he referred to as surface and source traits. Surface traits represent clusters of correlated variables and source traits represent the underlying structure of the personality. The later big Five Factor tests of the 1960s to 1990s are derivatives of Cattell's work (who kept updating the test as new insights were gained).

1956

AT&T, mimicking the example of the OSS/CIA, set up assessment centers to test executives.

1963

Building on Cattell, Tupes and Christal (1961) thoroughly established the five factors of personality testing as we know them today. Sadly, they published their results in an obscure Air Force publication that was not read by many in the psychology or academic communities. Warren T. Norman, however, did learn of Tupes and Christal's work. Norman (1963) replicated the Tupes and Christal study and confirmed the five-factor structure for trait taxonomy. A flurry of other personality researchers confirmed Norman's findings (Howard & Howard, 2000). During the 1960s and 1970s, traits were out of favor—only behaviors and situational responses were allowed. In 1981, a group reviewing available personality tests decided that most of the tests that held any promise seemed to measure a subset of five common factors, as Norman had previously claimed. These personality traits (commonly referred to as "Big Five" or "the five-factor model") are very common in business-oriented personality tests in use today. Throughout the 1980s and continuing through to the present, a plethora of personality researchers have established the Five-Factor Model as the basic paradigm for personality research. Four summaries of this research tradition are Goldberg (1993), Digman (1996), John, Angleitner, & Ostendorf (1988), and McCrae (1992).

1964

The Civil Rights Act is passed in 1964, followed by the Equal Employment Opportunity Act in 1972 and the American with Disabilities Act in 1990. These acts challenge traditional hiring practices, including the use of medically based tests.

1971

In a 1971 Supreme Court decision in the case of Griggs v. Duke Power, the court ruled that the Civil Rights Act of 1964 made certain forms of employee testing unconstitutional, particularly when there is a bias to the test. Many of the offbeat tests disappeared from widespread use. The Griggs decision did allow "the use of any professionally developed ability test, provided that it is not designed, intended, or used to discriminate." A later court decision that outlawed pre-employment polygraph tests pushed employers to use validated personality tests that measure reliability and honesty. Tests like the Cattell 16PF withstand all scrutiny.

1993

In a highly publicized case in 1993, Target stores agrees to pay more than $1 million to about 2,500 prospective security guards who objected to taking the Minnesota Multiphasic Personality Inventory, a test designed to assess mental patients.

2005

A court ruled in 2005 that Rent-A-Center Inc.'s use of a psychological assessment to screen candidates for management positions violated the Americans with Disabilities Act, which bans pre-employment medical examinations. In that case, brothers who worked for Rent-A-Center in Illinois filed a class-action suit objecting to the company's use of the Minnesota Multiphasic Personality Inventory test ("Hello, didn't you read about Target? It was in all the papers."). Although the company argued it gave the test to measure only personality traits, the court ruled that the testing violated the ADA because it could detect such conditions as depression and paranoia. What is a medical examination? Below is an excerpt from the EEOC, in the Disability-Related Inquiries and Medical Examinations of Employees section (which can be found at: www.eeoc.gov/policy/docs/guidance-inquiries.html#2).

> A "medical examination" is a procedure or test that seeks information about an individual's physical or mental impairments or health. The guidance on Pre-employment Questions and Medical Examinations lists the following factors that should be considered to determine whether a test (or procedure) is a medical examination: (1) whether the test is administered by a healthcare professional; (2) whether the test is interpreted by a healthcare professional; (3) whether the test is designed to reveal an impairment or physical or mental health; (4) whether the test is invasive; (5) whether the test measures an employee's performance of a task or measures his/her physiological responses to performing the task; (6) whether the test normally is given in a medical setting; and (7) whether medical equipment is used. In many cases, a combination of factors will be relevant in determining whether a test or procedure is a medical examination. In other cases, one factor may be enough to determine that a test or procedure is medical.

The historic and legal background of personality testing provides insight into the development of assessments and how to utilize them appropriately. In the following chapters, we will look at how to implement personality testing into the hiring process as well as to enhance communication and management style.

4

⁄⁄⁄ Screening Job Candidates

The Top Ten Hiring Mistakes and How to Avoid Them

THERE IS A very important book that we feel every hiring manager in business today should read. *You're Not the Person I Hired* is a guide that can make sure the person you bring into a critical job is, in fact, the person he or she appears to be.

According to this book, too often the hiring process is a case of mutually crossed fingers—both parties *hope* the match is a good one and *hope* the gamble they're taking will pay off. And then, regrettably, when Monday morning rolls around and the work begins, it all unravels.

Whose fault is it when the person who seemed like a fired-up go-getter turns out to be indifferent to goals she didn't set herself? Whose fault is it when the person hired to overhaul the organizational IT system turns out to be short-tempered, impractical, and a lousy communicator who alienates every functional department head? Whose fault is it when the new sales manager seems to have no impact whatsoever on penetrating two new markets—a mission-critical goal that he seemed fully capable of doing in interviews? *Whose fault is it when the person who shows up for the job isn't the person you thought you hired?*

"We believe the blame lies squarely with the hiring process itself, and we have compiled evidence to prove it," says Barry Deutsch, who wrote the book with Brad Remillard and Janet Boydell.

"Our research focusing on more than 20,000 hiring executives during the past fifteen years has identified the most common mistakes made in hiring," adds Deutsch. "Through the course of our analysis, we've determined the actual failure rate for newly hired managers and executives reaches a staggering 56% in many mid-sized and large organizations. We wanted to understand why. Prior to writing this book, we analyzed the hiring practices of 225 executive hires in 134 target companies."

What the three authors discovered was that almost every organization makes the same mistakes, over and over again. Most often, several mistakes occurred in each case. In nearly every situation, when new executives and managers failed to meet expectations, a major causal factor was that expectations had not been clearly defined in the first place.

Everything else fell out from there. Here are their ten most frequent mistakes, in reverse rank order:

10. *Desperation Hiring*: In 55% of searches, the hiring organization failed to budget enough time for the search, resulting in shallow sourcing and superficial interviews that failed to identify potential pitfalls.

9. *Ignoring Top Candidate's Needs*: 55% of searches were handled with a primary focus on the organization's needs and failed to build a compelling case for why top candidates should make the move.

8. *Failure to Probe for Core Success Factors*: The five best predictors of long-term success are self-motivation, leadership, comparable past performance, job-specific problem solving, and adaptability. A majority of searches failed to probe for these (56%).

7. *Fishing in Shallow Waters*: The search attracted only "Aggressive" candidates without seeking "Selective" and "Sleeper" candidates (62%).

6. *Performance Bias*: Interviews and offers were rewarded to the "best actor," not the best candidate (63%).

5. *Historical Bias:* The hiring company used only past performance to predict future results (68%).

4. *Snap Judgment*: Hiring teams relied too heavily on first impressions to make final hiring decisions (72%).

3. *Inappropriate "Prerequisites" Used Too Early in Selection Process*: Hiring teams placed too much emphasis on specific education, technical skills, and industry experience to screen out qualified candidates (76%).

2. *Superficial interviewing*: Candidates' backgrounds and claims were not deeply probed or verified (92%).

1. *Inadequate job descriptions* drove the hiring process; these focused solely on experience and skills, not company expectations. A staggering 93% of searches that resulted in new executive failure made this mistake at the outset.

The Causes of Hiring Mistakes

IN THEIR EXPERIENCE, the authors found that hiring mistakes are not caused by willful ignorance or negligence. Most often, new executive failure has several interrelated causes:

1. Inadequate preparation. Rarely had the hiring companies outlined a detailed, measurable definition of "success" that could be used to source, evaluate, and select candidates. Instead, they relied on outdated or insufficient job specs focused around desired attributes, educational attainment, and so on.

2. Lack of information. After the authors' work with the surveyed companies, nearly all the companies dramatically improved hiring practices and (most important) the performance of new hires. The authors concluded, therefore, that at least one cause of earlier hiring failures was not endemic organizational dysfunction, but a lack of information and training about how to hire more effectively at the executive level.

3. "Human nature." Interpersonal situations like interviews, conducted in a vacuum, are often guided primarily by gut feelings. Hiring team members who have not been trained to minimize these distractions are easily influenced by preconscious perceptions and nonverbal cues. When provided with a toolset designed to counterbalance these biases, interview team performance is far more likely to overcome distractions and focus on more critical success-based matters.

With the most common hiring mistakes and their causes in mind, they have developed and refined the Success Factor Methodology™ (for more information go to the Website www.impacthiringsolutions.com). This structured approach to executive hiring helps client companies prevent predictable, avoidable hiring pitfalls that plague many new-employee hires. The authors believe *every* organization—large or small, for-profit or nonprofit, public or private—is capable of using this methodology to significantly improve its hiring success at all levels of the organization.

There is only one way they've discovered to make sure the next employee you hire is successful: Tightly define what success will look like before the search begins, and focus like a laser beam on verifying whether each candidate you see has the demonstrated potential to create that success. The Success Factor Methodology requires a rethinking of almost every part of your hiring process. The progress you make will correlate directly with the amount of dedication, focus, leadership, and effort you expend. It works when *you* work—and there are no shortcuts.

⁕ *Stay Focused When the Finish Line Is in Sight*

You're Not The Person I Hired also covers that important time when the interview is over. The candidate has left the building.

"Now comes the hard part; making sense of what you've just heard," says Deutsch. "Assessment, verification, evaluation, and in-depth analysis of the candidate's stories and claims are on the docket for the interview team."

Do you have a systematic process to ensure the candidates have been truthful? How do you ensure you are continuing with the right candidate as you move through various interviews?

If you're like most hiring executives, when you interview a candidate, you scribbled a few notes in the resume margin. You formed a general impression based on a mélange of nonverbal cues and behaviors. You've already decided that you "like" or "don't like" the candidate. But you don't have a tool to help you compare apples to apples, and candidates to your Success Factor Snapshot.

☙ *The Water Cooler Is No Place to Debrief*

THE AUTHORS HAVE frequently seen interviewers emerge from a round of interviews and then commiserate near the proverbial water cooler.

> ➤ *"So, what did you think of Candidate A?"*
> ➤ *"Well, he seemed enthusiastic."*
> ➤ *"She had a lot of energy."*
> ➤ *"He was polite."*
> ➤ *"Seemed okay. I think he could probably do the job."*

These abstract impressions are not grounded in what's needed to succeed on the job. A case in point from the authors' experience: One of the best people a client of theirs ever hired nearly wasn't invited back for a second interview. She was a powerhouse—highly accomplished, with more than enough demonstrable success behind her. In terms of her ability to do the job, she stood head and shoulders above all other candidates.

There was, however, a "problem." The candidate was not a fashion plate. The company's employees tended to be fashionable, with name-brand labels oozing out of every office suite. The candidate arrived at the first interview in a tasteful but conservative suit, her hair pulled back in a plain style, wearing minimal makeup. Some members of the interview panel (they never asked who, exactly) apparently fixated on her "lack of grooming."

When Deutsch spoke to the hiring team after the first interview and they expressed reluctance to continue interviewing the candidate, he was puzzled. It took considerable probing to uncover the fact that the interviewers who had expressed reservations were subconsciously prejudiced based on the candidate's "stodgy, plain" clothing and makeup.

However, the position was not one that required interfacing with clients who would expect flash and style. She would be managing sophisticated financial analysis, planning, budgeting, and forecasting.

Here was a candidate with phenomenal qualifications who had nailed the answer to every question they gave her—but she wasn't "glam" enough?

Deutsch let the hiring committee know what a mistake they were making. The important question, he reminded them, was not whether this candidate subscribed to *Vogue* and *Elle*, shopped at Saks, or invested a fifth of her income in facials, French manicures, MAC makeup, or triple-foil highlights. The important question—the only question—was whether she could do what the company needed done.

The hiring team rethought their position. The candidate was invited back, eventually offered the job, promoted twice, and last they knew, was still successfully making things happen nearly a decade later, Armani suit or no.

This episode crystallizes a universal truth about candidate evaluation: *Superficial, irrelevant issues often get more of an interviewer's attention than real substance.*

◆ *"Criteria" to Toss Out*

WHEN YOU INTERVIEW, what's on your mental checklist? Some of the most time-honored "criteria" have absolutely nothing to do with whether a candidate can do the job.

- ➤ Strong presentation
- ➤ Assertive or aggressive
- ➤ Manicured
- ➤ Polished shoes in the right color (brown with navy, not black)
- ➤ "Enthusiasm"
- ➤ High energy
- ➤ Good eye contact
- ➤ Strong handshake
- ➤ Well-spoken
- ➤ Instant, unhesitant recall of events from many years ago (honestly, if somebody asked you about something that happened in 1993, wouldn't you pause and look up to the right as you tried to remember all the details?)
- ➤ Smooth speech without "ums" or stutters or backtracking
- ➤ Personable

Many hiring mistakes occur because the hiring team draws first impressions from factors like these, or because the candidate either wowed them or bored them during interviews. The team can lose sight of the real goal: measuring the candidate's ability to deliver the results defined in the success factor worksheet.

"You're not hiring an actor," says Deutsch. "You're hiring an operations director, or a VP of finance, or a plant manager. In what way, exactly, does a candidate's handshake correlate with their ability to succeed in those jobs?"

In some jobs, of course, presentation skills and a solid professional appearance are important. But focusing on "hot-button" factors like those in the list above does not help to select the right candidate.

✤ *The Eight-Dimension Success Matrix™*

To ELIMINATE INTERVIEWERS' ingrained tendency to focus on superficial criteria and miss substantive evidence, they developed a structured tool to help each interviewer evaluate each candidate—objectively, fairly, and comprehensively.

The Eight-Dimension Success Matrix is the tool the authors of *You're Not The Person I Hired* have their clients use to rate "fit" based on the examples, illustrations, specifics, results, accomplishments, and patterns of behavior that emerge in candidate interviews.

It is quick to use, easy to understand, and focused on the job itself. Perhaps most importantly, it calibrates interviewer ratings, keeping everyone on the same page. Built around the five key predictors of success, the Eight-Dimension Success Matrix forces interviewers to assess answers to questions in a uniform way.

Accountability to the group is vital. When interviewers know they will have to justify the ratings assigned to each candidate to the entire group of interviewers—especially if they've designated Candidate A's Team Leadership ability 1 while everybody else assigned her a 2—the whole process is taken more seriously.

Because each member of the interviewing team fills out an Eight-Dimension Success Matrix form after each interview, by end of a long interview cycle a candidate's file may contain twenty or more forms. The full file allows the person with final hiring power to evaluate a full spectrum of data on all Success Factors. Skimming the right column helps the hiring executive to rapidly compare the same candidate interview-to-interview and also to evaluate candidates' qualifications against each other on equal footing. For more information on the Eight-Dimension Success Matrix form, go to the Website www.impacthiringsolutions.com.

◆ When References Go Bad

IF A CANDIDATE makes it to the second round of interviews, it's getting serious. You've settled on one or possibly two candidates. You believe with all your heart, soul, and mind that one is the right person for the job. He or she seems to be the cherry on the sundae, and you're looking forward to making the job offer to the number one candidate.

You phone HR and tell them to make two quick reference calls based on names and numbers the candidate has given you. Once that's done, you figure, it's a wrap. Stop right there.

Even though most reference calls tend to be five-minute, rubber stamp, "Is-he-a-nice-guy / would-you-rehire-her / did-she-do-well" conversations, *yours* will not be. Your calls won't even technically be "reference calls." They will be twenty to thirty minutes long. They will go into great detail. They will be deep third-party verifications of what the candidate has told you in the interviews. You will push and probe for nearly as much detail with each reference as you did with the candidate.

You must do so, not because you do not trust this person (it's obvious that you do, or you wouldn't be on the cusp of offering him a job), but because verification is a mandatory step in a proven hiring process. Ordinary reference calls (and even background checks—more on that in a moment) don't get to the heart of potential problems. Most people who receive reference calls expect to be on the line for fewer than ten minutes. They expect to be able to say simple things like, "Cathy is a great worker! You can't go wrong hiring her. I'd rehire her in an instant."

But you, as the hiring company, are about to invest literally hundreds of thousands of dollars in a new hire. To do so without fully verifying what the candidate has told you would be irresponsible. Up until now, you've had only the candidate's word to go on. References, though, are a treasure chest waiting to be opened and explored.

⚜ *Finding the Right Reference*

IRST OFF: No family, friends, or personal references. While many applicants still include these in their list, personally invested people are unlikely to yield much useful information. When a reference's primary relationship with a candidate is personal, there is an automatic conflict of interest. Their loyalty is to the candidate, not you, and most importantly, they are unlikely to be able to speak intelligently about the candidate's work accomplishments.

Once you've decided you want to hire a particular candidate, ask them for three to five professional references. Ideally, these should be former bosses, peers, or individuals they have supervised. The authors suggest to their search clients that reference checks should be conducted on a 360-degree basis, including all the individuals who might touch this person, both inside and outside the company. Ask for the numbers of key customers, vendors, and suppliers.

If the candidate is still employed at a company where they have been for a long time (five years or more), and they would prefer you do not contact their boss until an offer is made, work around it as best you can. Perhaps a former mentor from another department has left the company and would be able to speak about them. Maybe the person who hired them originally and saw them through their meteoric rise first few years is now retired and living in Key West—call her.

A Top 5% candidate, if he or she is interested in the job, will work with you on this and may even agree to let you contact a current employer under certain circumstances. As a last resort, sometimes candidates will grant you permission to talk with their boss once an offer is formally presented. You can always make the offer contingent upon the successful outcome of reference checks.

Because coworkers and colleagues have usually spent more time with the candidate than the boss, they are outstanding sources of verification. Usually "lateral" references can offer deeper insights into work style, team leadership ability, personality, and cultural issues. Pay particular attention to these areas when speaking to former coworkers, probing for any indications that the person may pose interpersonal problems or "rub people the wrong way."

✤ *Going Deeper: Secondary References*

DON'T STOP AT the first layer of verification. When you speak to first-tier references (those whose names the candidate gave you), ask *whom else* the candidate worked with, reported to, supervised, or led as part of a team. These are secondary references, and they are additional potential sources of objective verification.

Then, go back to the candidate and ask them whether they would mind if you contacted these secondary references. A highly qualified candidate will usually agree immediately.

If you sense hesitation, it may be a red flag. If the candidate objects to contacting a secondary reference, ask why. Sometimes they will offer a good reason (*"I was charged with supervising the team's efforts. His department was always late with their deliverables and I had to ride him hard for a year to make sure he followed up on his commitments. I don't think Judy, my primary reference, was aware of the ongoing friction between their departments, but Bob in accounting was on the same team. Would you like me to put you in touch with him?"*). Other times, they will be vague and evasive (*"Um, well, we didn't work together much and she didn't have anything to do with my projects. I don't think she'd really be able to tell you much."*). Listen carefully to the answers you receive from the candidate and make an informed judgment call before proceeding with a secondary reference verification interview.

As a rule of thumb, if you get strong verification not only from a candidate's "first tier" of references, but also from secondary references, you can almost bet the farm you've found the candidate you're seeking. (Almost. See "Background Checks" before you leap, though.)

Finally, it is important not to "wear out" references. Third-party verification calls should be one of the last items on the hiring agenda, not the first. Not even the middle. The Eight-Point Success Validation form is lengthy and intense and will take at least thirty minutes to complete; this is a significant investment of time, and you should let people know up front that the call will take this long.

A good third of the information you need about candidates is obtained in verification phone calls. It's best to set expectations early in a reference phone call. Make it clear that you are *not* asking for a recommendation. Rather, you are verifying information that you've been given, and you would appreciate as much detail as the reference feels comfortable giving.

❧ *The Vital Role of Testing and Assessment*

T HE AUTHORS OF *You're Not the Person I Hired* strongly believe testing is a valuable adjunct to the Success Factor Methodology, because when administered correctly, tests can uncover useful information about personality traits, potential for high achievement, and other factors that may not be immediately evident in an interview situation. However, there are several cautions about assessment instruments.

"We highly recommend that our clients use an outside, third-party assessment professional who is specifically trained to select appropriate tests, as well as administer and interpret the results," says Deutsch.

Beyond using appropriate personnel, they advise the following:

1. **The instrument must be appropriate to the job.** Each selected test should measure traits, characteristics, and skills that are directly and obviously relevant to the job. Appropriate scales may be honesty and integrity—important qualities for the person who will be in charge of the company coffers. On the other hand, there is no apparent reason to administer an instrument like the Minnesota Multiphasic Personality Inventory, which is designed to test for mental and emotional disorders.

2. **The instrument must be valid and reliable.** The Buros Institute, an organization founded in 1935 to catalog and evaluate psychological tests, publishes two comprehensive directories that can help you select instruments known to be reliable and valid. *The Mental Measurements Yearbook* and *Tests in Print* are available at most libraries and contain descriptions and reviews of psychological instruments. Be sure to ask consulting industrial psychologists whether the assessments they use are listed in these directories. If you are interested in how they were developed and validated, you can consult these reference works. At last count, the volumes had collected development, price, administration, and interpretation data on more than 11,000 instruments.

3. **Be wary of free online tests.** Unless they come from a highly regarded institute and/or are listed in one of the books mentioned above, they may not be valid and reliable instruments.

4. **The instrument must be administered and interpreted professionally.** It cannot emphasized enough that tests, inventories, personal-

ity profiles, and the like are difficult to interpret for a nonprofessional. Human resources professionals are generally not qualified to administer psychological or behavioral tests. If you do choose to use some form of assessment to help you make a hiring decision, it is safer and more effective to delegate responsibility to a third party, who will likely ask candidates to sign waivers before taking the tests. These professionals will also ensure that untrained people on the hiring team do not focus on one or two potentially "negative" findings in a twenty-page report—something they have seen frequently.

✸ A Comprehensive Background Check

FINALLY, WE REACH the granddaddy of all pre-hiring due diligence: the background check. As with psychological and personality testing, the authors believe this is an activity best left to trained professionals who understand the legal and ethical constraints of such activities.

Background checks are often the last shield between a hiring company and a particularly slick candidate who interviews well. You might be surprised at how many people misrepresent their educational credentials, for example. In recent years, the media has exposed numerous scandals resulting from puffery in nearly every sector.

> ➤ In 2004, Quincy Troupe, poet laureate of the State of California and a tenured college professor, resigned his post. The reason? He had lied for years about his background, listing himself as a graduate of Grambling University. In fact, the professor (who was in charge of training graduate students, among other duties) had never even finished a bachelor's degree.

> ➤ Jeffrey Papows, former president of Lotus Software, was revealed by a 1999 *Wall Street Journal* investigation to have habitually exaggerated his past and accomplishments. While he claimed to be an orphan who rose through military ranks to eventually earn a Ph.D. from Pepperdine, he in fact had parents living in Massachusetts and a Ph.D. from a correspondence school. (He did, however, have a Master's from Pepperdine.)

> ➤ Sandra Baldwin, former president of the United States Olympic Committee, resigned after admitting that she had lied on her resume about earning a Ph.D. from Arizona State University. She had not.

> ➤ Joseph Ellis, a Pulitzer Prize-winning biographer and professor of history at Mt. Holyoke College, was immensely popular for courses that included his personal insights into the violence and mayhem he had witnessed in Vietnam. In 2001, however, the *Boston Globe* exposed him: Dr. Ellis had never left the States during the Vietnam War.

> ➤ In 2002, Veritas Software lost its chief financial officer, Kenneth Lonchar, who resigned after his employer found out he had lied about his education, including an MBA from Stanford. He never earned such a degree. The company's stock plummeted in the weeks following these revelations.

"There are many more cases like these," says Deutsch. "They could fill ten pages with just *recent* examples of resume-padding gone horribly wrong. Obviously all these people were highly accomplished, but their basic dishonesty about degrees and other background information introduced high levels of doubt about their overall ethics and trustworthiness."

If such visible and respected organizations can be successfully bluffed in their highest-level hires, it can happen to your organization, too. The only way to be sure everything you've heard is true is to invest the time and money to verify the candidate's claims on his resume or other documents he completes and signs after beginning the interviewing process.

Many third-party providers can run a comprehensive background check to make sure there are no skeletons in any closet. These companies are fully up-to-date on laws that regulate the extent to which such checks can be used prior to employment.

If you decide to wait to run these checks until after you extend an offer, be sure you make the offer contingent upon satisfactory results from the background check.

1. Criminal Background. In rare cases, charming and charismatic characters who just happen to be crooks have made their way all the way into positions of power. In the authors' own experience, they know of a candidate who was offered a position as CFO without a criminal check. It was revealed later—too late—that he was under active investigation by the FBI and had allegedly embezzled huge sums of money in the past. A criminal background check would have revealed these issues before the company hired him, no matter how charming and convincing he had been in interviews.

2. Credit. For any candidate who will be placed in a role where they will have access to the company coffers (or even something as innocent as a company credit card), the authors strongly recommend a credit check. Does the person have a huge amount of debt in the form of mortgages and consumer debt? Does the person make their required payments in a timely manner? Has the person filed for bankruptcy? What is their credit score? The authors realize that nobody is perfect, and while a high level of debt does not automatically disqualify a candidate, nor does the occasional late payment, there is merit in being cautious and checking these items. Financial pressure and stress can cause even the most well-intentioned people to snap. Knowing a high-level executive's financial straits up front can help to head off potential problems.

3. Educational Background. It may not actually be important to the job whether somebody earned an MBA or simply attended a year of a program without finishing. However, dishonesty about educational achievement is a huge red flag that should cause you to dig much deeper in every other area. If a candidate lies about this accomplishment, what else might he or she be lying about? Because educational background is frequently misrepresented, this check is the most likely place where you will uncover discrepancies. Integrity matters. The authors never recommend going forward with a candidate who has lied about their education.

4. State Drivers' License Bureau. If a candidate has a record of arrests for driving under the influence, reckless accidents, or other egregious traffic violations, it may be a hint of deeper problems—and potential liability or risk to the company.

5. Social Security Verification. Social Security will identify the names associated with the candidate's Social Security number. While most discrepancies can be cleared up quickly (marriage or adoption changed the last name, or a religious conversion changed the entire name), multiple aliases may be a red flag and should be explained by the candidate.

5

⫸ Cracking the Code

The Eight Ways to Gain True Insight into Personality

The Personics Factor Matrix™

WHAT REALLY MAKES people tick?
The short answer is there is no one thing that can explain personality. Human beings are complex, and you need to take that complexity into account when you are hiring and managing.

You have probably heard of the ancient Indian parable of the blind men and the elephant. In this fable an Indian Rajah brought together all of the blind men in the land to examine an elephant. None knew what an elephant was and were eager to find out.

Each blind man was allowed to touch a different part of the elephant. One felt the head, another the trunk, while the rest laid their hands on the tusk, ear, leg, flank, tail and tuft and so on. When asked by the Rajah what type of thing an elephant is, the blind man who felt the trunk said it was like a snake. No, said the one who grasped the smooth and pointed ivory tusk, an elephant is like a spear. You've got it wrong, said the man who felt the leg, and elephant is like a pillar. The man who touched the flank said that can't be, an elephant is like a wall. And so the argument went.

While the blind men were accurate in describing what they touched, none were correct in presenting the correct generalized view of an elephant. That is because they all had obtained very useful but insufficient data.

Two questions generally come up, and you may already be asking yourself the first: How many data points are sufficient? A second question that comes up is, how do you keep it all straight?

Let's tackle the first question. When it comes to cracking the personality code, we recommend that you get eight different views of the elephant. Personality assessment should not be based on a single issue or observation. While saying someone has "a great personality" is a compliment, it is not really helpful for hiring and managing. You need many more data points to construct an accurate moving picture of a complex personality.

The same is true when it comes to hiring and managing people. Have you ever seen the individual frames of a motion picture reel? Each frame gives you a picture in time. To paraphrase one psychology textbook, the data we collect during the process of personality assessment is useful only to the extent that we can translate the "snapshots" derived from each tool into an accurate "moving picture" of the person (Beutler and Berren, *Integrative Assessment of Adult Personality*, 1995).

Here are the eight pieces of the puzzle you will want to examine:

1. Compare their resume against your job description.*

2. Assess their problem-solving resources.

3. Determine their patterns for coping with stress.

4. Examine their interpersonal interaction styles.

5. Analyze career activity interests.

6. Assess how they respond to tests.

7. Chronicle strengths and weakness ledger.

8. Create probing personality interview questions.*

*Steps 1 and 8 are for use in assessing hiring candidates; steps 2–7 are used for hiring and managing.

Now let's tackle the second question: how do you keep it all straight? That is why we developed the following matrix. Regardless of the tools you use, we believe there is a best practices methodology to follow to fully understand what makes someone tick.

⧻ *The Personics Factor Matrix™*

T O ELIMINATE A manager's natural tendency to focus on the likeability of the person, we developed a structured tool to help you objectively and comprehensively evaluate personality. The Personics Factor Matrix™ is the tool we have our clients use to gain insight into the personality of a candidate during the hiring process.

Of course, we advocate that you use the most sophisticated assessments possible and use trained professionals to help you evaluate personality traits. However, lacking that, this tool will even help organize perceptions when you use even the most rudimentary assessment instruments.

The Personics Factor Matrix™

Name			Date	
Position/Title:				

Critical Step	Looking for...	Helps to...	Rank the Fit (High, Medium or Low)
1. Compare their resume against your job description	For hiring, evidence they have done work like this in the past	Determine if their personality has been drawn to this type of work	
2. Assess their problem-solving resources	Usual approaches for resolving problems	Get a picture of their strengths for solving most problems	
3. Determine their patterns for coping with stress	The person's "core wiring" for dealing with stress and pressure	Understand how they will react to conflict, opposition, and emotionally charged events	
4. Examine their interpersonal interaction styles	How they deal with others	Learn what their major sources of satisfaction are when building relationships	
5. Analyze career activity interests	Career activity interests and occupational interest patterns	Understand their thought-flow process	
6. Assess how they respond to tests	Are they showing their true personality or answering in an idealistic fashion?	Make sure they are not answering the test in an untruthful or inconsistent manner	
7. Chronicle strengths and weakness ledger	A two-sided ledger, with 4–6 strengths on one side and 4–6 weaknesses on the other side	Quickly compare the strong points and the corresponding weak points	
8. Create personality probing interview questions	For hiring, areas of concern	Probe for more information to clarify how the person will behave on the job	

1. Compare Their Resume against Your Job Description

Sounds obvious, doesn't it? Surprising how easy it is to blow right past this step in the hiring process. The wrong hiring decision can cost your company well over two to three times the individual's salary, according to executive recruiters, Barry Deutsch and Brad Remillard (2005, *You're Not the Person I Hired: A CEO's Guide to Hiring Top Talent*). This figure might be a conservative estimate because of factors like training, evaluation, termination, and re-initiating the hiring process and lost opportunity costs. So it pays to scrutinize.

Past experience alone is not what you are looking for when you review the resume. You are looking at how well they performed, what were their successes, and how adaptable they might be to the job that needs to be done for your organization. Experience is nice, but it is results that really count.

2. Assess Their Problem-Solving Resources

Is this person a problem solver? And if so, what kind of problem solver? Each of us has unique problem-solving resources on which we rely. You will want to determine what the person's strengths are when it comes to problem solving and learning new skills. What are the usual approaches this person will use to resolve these problems? How do they best learn new information?

3. Determine Their Patterns for Coping with Stress

Stress is a force that tends to distort the body, a factor that induces bodily or mental tension, or an automatic physical reaction to a danger or demand in the environment. As one physician stated, "Stress is any demand, either internal, external or both, that causes us to mentally and physically readjust in order to maintain a sense of balance within our life."

Without a doubt, stress is a fact of life in today's work world. So, determining a candidate's or employee's ability to cope with stress is critical for a manager. However, we don't recommend that you put candidates or employees through cooked-up stress tests to see how they cope under pressure (like asking a job candidate to open a window that has been nailed shut).

Some causes of stress include:

➢ Fear of failure.

➢ Making mistakes.

> ➢ Fear of rejection.

> ➢ Changes like loss, money, illness, injury, career and more.

> ➢ Unrealistic expectations from self and others.

> ➢ Life pressures like deadlines or taxes (April 15 causes a lot of stress in the U.S.).

As Stewart Emory once said: "The absence of fear is not an option that is available to most people. People are looking for that, but that is just not an option. The difference between people who are really making it in the world and the people who are not is simple: The people who are making it in the world are making it and they have fear."

4. Examine Their Interpersonal Interaction Styles

Breakdowns in communication are never good for an organization. So take a good look at the individual's style for relating and communicating with others. How do they usually react in dealing with others? What is their comfort level in interacting and personal connection with others? Personality assessments can tell you the person's major sources of gratification and satisfaction when building relationships with each other.

This is the time to identify potential red flags. A personality assessment can discover issues that are sometimes overlooked during the traditional interviewing process and can quantify a hunch or feeling the interviewer may have about a particular candidate. Knowing interpersonal interaction styles can also help understand how to manage individuals for greater work performance. A comparison of the interpersonal dynamics of teams, departments, employees, and candidates is well worth the effort.

5. Analyze Career Activity Interests

Certain personality tests help you gain information that may either support the person's present career choices or assist them to explore, consider, and plan for another career direction. This is not to say you will be recommending another career choice to someone you are considering hiring or currently managing. Rather, you are using this information to determine fit. All organizations want to ensure that they have the right people in the right positions and effectively distribute these human assets and talents. Here are the seven career patterns to look for:

Analyzing: Investigating, observing and solving problems of a business, cultural, scientific, or social nature that requires the use of ideas, words and symbols to uncover new facts or theories—activity characteristic of people who enjoy working in laboratory and research settings, the mathematics field, and the life science, medical science, physical science, and social science professions. They usually find greater satisfaction being involved with the challenge of work that requires conceptual thinking and analysis of quantitative problems than work requiring extensive interaction with people in group projects.

Creating: Bringing creative self-expression into art forms, literature, or innovative products and services—activity characteristic of people who find satisfaction working in the artistic, literary, drama, musical and performing arts fields. They usually value activities that enable them to express their abilities, ideas, and talents, especially those which bear the imprint of their efforts.

Helping: Solving problems through discussions with others, and encouraging relationships between people so as to help and develop others to live a full, satisfying life—activity characteristic of people who find satisfaction working in the healthcare, religious, social service, or educational professions. They usually enjoy working in groups, sharing responsibilities, and having opportunities to be helpful, nurturing, and caring for others, especially if people require some sort of assistance, training or education.

Influencing: Convincing, directing, or persuading others to attain organizational goals and/or economic gain—activity characteristic of people who find satisfaction working on the sales, marketing, and management aspects of business or in the professions of consulting, law, and politics. They usually enjoy having the opportunity to exercise control over matters important to them, to have some degree of influence over people, and to work in situations where they can make decisions and persuade others to their viewpoints in the effort to get things accomplished.

Organizing: Initiating procedures, managing projects, and directly supervising the work of others—activity characteristic of people who enjoy working in situations whereby they can handle the details of organizational productivity, data systems, and accuracy of information processing. They usually find satisfaction solving day-to-day problems to bring orderliness to situations, planning budgets and cash flow, and handling investments.

Producing: Accomplishing tasks of an orderly and systematic nature through the use of machines, materials, objects, or tools—activity characteristic of people working in the construction, farming, and the manual/skilled trades. They usually prefer situations where they can work with their hands, be outdoors, and see the visible results of their efforts.

Venturing: Being involved in situations and tasks that require physical endurance, competing with others, and some degree of risk-taking—activity characteristic of people who enjoy involvement in athletics, working in the military/law enforcement professions, and participating in risky and adventurous events. They usually get satisfaction from competing with others whereby they have opportunities to win individually and/or by working with others on a team. They often seek out excitement and are generally quite confident of their physical abilities and skills.

6. Assess How They Respond to Tests

You should also use tests with scales for what is known as "impression management." This is necessary in order to understand the accuracy of results and whether someone is trying to "fake good" or misrepresent themselves. A critical element in predicting a potential candidate's success is measuring real personality and style in an interview. An in-depth work style and personality assessment presents a fairly accurate picture of a candidate's personality, work style, and fit within a company's culture.

If a profile does not have an impression management scale, then it is difficult to tell how accurate the data is. A profile needs to have at least 164 questions in order to gather enough data for this scale.

7. Chronicle Strengths and Weakness Ledger

Benjamin Franklin reportedly had a decision-making process when he was faced with important challenges. Franklin divided a sheet of paper into two columns, and on the left side listed the reasons for doing something and on the right side the reasons against. Much like a bank ledger with credits and debits, this simple tool greatly aided the analysis of information. Often a quick scan of the two lists gave him the information he needed to make the right choice.

We recommend you do the same for the personality of a job candidate or an employee under your supervision. Like a bank ledger, every credit should have a corresponding debit. That is because for every strength a person possesses there tends to be a corresponding weakness. Being assertive is a strength; however, that personality can be too assertive and off-putting for some people. This can assist in understanding the person better. Your list might look something like this:

Strengths:	Weaknesses:
➤ Assertive	➤ Can be too assertive for some people
	➤ Some concern of how others may view them.
➤ Bold & expressive	➤ May be too chatty at times.
➤ Perfectionist	➤ Can be rigid in how some things are handled
➤ Rule-conscious	➤ It can be hard for this person to make exceptions to the rules
➤ Spontaneous	➤ Can make decisions too quickly
➤ Traditional	➤ More comfortable with traditional methods
	➤ A concrete thinker

8. Create Personality Probing Interview Questions

So, what have you learned about the job candidate so far through personality assessments? What remains to learn? To find out, develop interview questions that probe facets of the personality on which you need more details.

Forget those old standby questions like, "Tell me about your strengths and weaknesses." Instead, let's say you wanted to determine how they cope with stress. You might ask candidates to give an example of when they made a terrible mistake and how they handled it. Ask them how they think others perceive them when they are under stress. For making a mistake, did they blame others or take responsibility for the outcome? Listen for their process. Do they ask for help? Watch body language and tone of voice to see how much insecurity the candidate expresses at the idea of making a mistake or having stress.

As consultants trained in psychology, this is something we help our clients create for new candidates. To help you create questions, here are some sample preliminary interview questions for a candidate. Naturally, these are not meant to be questions to ask all candidates, but are indicative of the types of questions you might ask.

➤ What process do you think helps you to learn? Give an example of how you learn a very complex system or skill and what your process was.

➤ How would you handle a situation that brought up many different changes? How do you like to see change take place? Give an example when change was implemented and it just didn't work out.

- Have you ever worked with individuals who are abstract thinkers? How did you deal with that kind of thought process?

- Give an example of when you have had to make an exception to the guidelines or rules. How have you handled that?

- How have you handled a situation where you had to take a chance on something?

✦ *In Summary*

WHEW, SEEMS LIKE a lot to worry about. Just remember, personality tests are a standard recruiting practice for many branches of the government and military, as well as Fortune 500 companies when assessing potential hires for key or critical positions. This is not guesswork or an untested science.

As with any business decision, having and organizing the right information is critical. In-depth work style and personality assessment testing can provide insight into potential hires, as well as the current workforce. The trick is to gather the information and then look at it in an organized fashion.

Part Three

Managing by Personality

6

⁇ This Is Only a Test

Connected Managing by Personality Traits

"Watch your words: they become your thoughts.
Watch your thoughts: they become your actions.
Watch your actions: they become your habits.
Watch your habits: they become your destiny."

Frank Outlaw

PERSONALITY TESTS NOT only help when hiring, they just might be a manager's best tool to connect with employees.

You can manage the hard way or the easy way, the choice is up to you. The hard way is to be the "my way or the highway" type of boss. You know the kind, always forcing workers to do things in a way that isn't natural for them. Wouldn't it be better to use your understanding of personality traits to tap into the natural flow so you can get the best out of your people? Of course, knowing your employees, understanding their concerns, and developing connected relationships with them should be the normal procedure for all managers.

What is the payoff to a manager for developing connected relationships with employees using personality assessments? Here are three good benefits. First, it enables the manager to better anticipate what roadblocks might occur with a worker, and what to try to reduce this resistance. Second, understanding where employees are coming from will help you plan out how much participation you need from them and will give some clues as to how change should be communicated to them. Third, creating connected relationships builds commitment and loyalty.

⚕ *Take the Connected Leader Test*

Ｈow connected are you as a manager? To find out, we asked our colleague Dr. Bruce Heller, an industrial psychologist with twenty years experience and author of *The Prodigal Executive—How to Coach Executives Too Painful to Keep, Too Valuable to Fire*, to help us design a quick connected leader self-test. For each of the ten questions, choose the response that best matches your situation. Then give yourself the corresponding point value for each question. Total up your score and look to the end of the test for how to interpret your score.

Connected Leader Test *Questions*	*Scoring instructions:* **Don't know = 1 point** **Never = 2 points** **Seldom = 3 points** **Often = 4 points** **Always = 5 points**
1. Do you get personally involved with co-workers, colleagues, peers, and others?	
2. Do you believe that your role as a leader is to serve your direct reports?	
3. Do you feel your employees are motivated to help you achieve your goals?	
4. How often do you acknowledge a special occasion of a direct report?	
5. Do you reflect upon the potential impact you make on direct reports?	
6. Do you spend time thinking about meeting the needs of others?	
7. Do you consider yourself a sensitive leader?	
8. In your family, did your parents spend time listening and reflecting on an emotional level?	
9. Do you think your peers and direct reports consider you a sensitive leader?	
10. Do you keep a journal of your interactions and conversations?	
TOTAL	

Scoring

This self-test helps you identify what level of connected leader you are. Research has shown that leaders who are able to attend and connect with their employees are more successful. This is because connection creates a depth of relationship that translates into improved productivity, less turnover, and a more engaged work force.

Here are the breakdowns for your scoring. If you scored:

0–14

You are disconnected from the people who make up your organization. To become more connected, you may need to hire an executive coach.

15–26

Your connections are frail and therefore you could benefit from taking more time to think about others and find ways to connect with them. Sharing something about yourself will be effective. Also, begin to keep a journal of your interactions. Think about ways you can become more connected to people in your organization.

27–36

You are a connected leader. This means that you connect with your team and work towards building relationships. However, you could benefit from being even more connected by spending time walking around and speaking to people and especially beginning to share with people something about you personally. This can mean a hobby or an interest.

36–50

You are deeply connected as a leader. You have an ability to think about ways to communicate and be sensitive to the needs of the people in your organization. Therefore, people want to work for you and you have a loyal following.

❧ *How to Get Connected*

IT'S BEEN SAID there is a significant difference between hearing someone speak to you and really listening to what they say. Most managers consider themselves to be good listeners. But is that really the case?

Being a connected manager requires that you suspend judgment of your subordinates' actions or reactions while you try to understand them. Personality assessments provide a great deal of clues. Sometimes, you will need to read between the lines of what they say. Next comes gentle questioning and probing to clarify what is going on. The goal is to understand and not to judge.

For most managers, this does not come naturally. These tips will help you become a better listener and a more connected leader.

1. Practice active listening. An active listener is ready and willing to really hear what the other person has to say. When you actively listen, you pay close attention to the speaker and don't just wait until they get done talking, or worse yet, interrupt them. Paraphrase back to the person to check that you fully understand what is being said.

2. Enter the listening zone. When a subordinate approaches you to discuss something, go into listening mode. Do what it takes to minimize distractions, look the speaker in the eye, and make a decision in your head to listen. If you know their personality type, then think what their style of communication is.

3. Seek to understand first. Pay close attention to what the subordinate is saying, both the words and the feeling behind them. Watch the speaker's body language. Instead of interrupting if you have a question or comment, write it down so you can remember it for later.

4. Show empathy. Empathy—the ability to know and feel what others experience—is the foundation of being a connected leader. Managers in industries ranging from healthcare to high-tech are realizing benefits to their team's productivity when they show empathy. The old adage applies: "They don't care how much you know until they know how much you care."

5. Hold your reactions. Have you ever seen someone react negatively to what you say without saying a word? Even if you disagree with the subordinate, do not react negatively by shaking your head or putting on a big frown. Instead give positive cues like smiling, maintaining eye contact, leaning toward the speaker, taking notes, and even making those little positive "right" and "go on" statements. When they are finished, take a breath and then weigh in with your feedback.

We all want to be understood. Employee buy-in comes when a manager is able to listen attentively, understand them as people, and lead naturally.

❧ *People Do Things for Their Own Reasons*

A BOOK WE RECOMMEND is *Managing People: What's Personality Got to Do With It* by Carol Ritberger, Ph.D. (www.ritberger.com). She surmises that success in life is significantly, if not totally, dependent upon our ability to manage.

We manage on the job, we manage in our governmental and educational institutions, and we manage in our personal lives. According to Dr. Ritberger, successful managers are those who understand what needs to be accomplished, who communicate with those who are supposed to get it done, and achieve a desired result through their efforts.

"In trying to understand human behavior, there's a basic principle that applies to all our actions: People do things for their reasons and not ours," says Dr. Ritberger. "Another way to say it is: Other people see things, respond, and react in different ways. They'll usually do what they think will offer them the greatest reward for their efforts."

What this means, continues Dr. Ritberger, is that no one in a position of power can motivate others to work unless they understand which motivation factors produce the results they seek.

"Sure, people will make a halfhearted effort if they're threatened, but all this does is produce marginal results, and it also ends up creating frustration, resentment, rebellious behavior, and power struggles," she says.

According to Dr. Ritberger, a good manager knows that people need to feel accepted for who they are, long to be recognized for their contributions, and want to enjoy themselves when interacting with their peers or superiors. A wise supervisor remembers the importance of the individual and knows that when folks feel good about themselves, they'll naturally reach higher standards in their performance and be motivated for their reasons and not yours. An intelligent person uses this information to help others become more productive and effective in what they do.

Dr. Ritberger believes that as you seek to understand more about personality, it's helpful to keep these three important factors in mind:

1. People want to fit in, and as a result will take on what they perceive to be the behavior norm for their environment, even if it isn't in alignment with their personality boundaries.

2. It's human nature to judge people based on first impressions that may not reflect the true nature of their personalities.

3. There's a natural tendency to compare other people's behavior with our own to determine whether their personality is compatible with ours.

"However, if you understand that personality is more than what you see on the surface, then you'll have the opportunity to really get to know new acquaintances and discover their natural talents," says Dr. Ritberger. "You may realize that someone you misread initially is exactly who you've been seeking for a job, or is most compatible in a social relationship. You might even find yourself more appreciative of the differences in people because you'll recognize that their strengths are your weaknesses, and how those variations offer the greatest opportunity to create a dynamic team of self-motivated people."

⚜ *How to Understand Yourself*

BEFORE YOU USE personality assessments to manage others, you should also use them to better understand yourself. Teamwork is about how people work with each other, and personality types play a big role in this. The first step is to know yourself. Here are some thoughts to help you as a manager with that process.

Have you ever looked carefully at a seed? It's really amazing to see what is in a little seed, and that may help us to learn more about what is inside of us. For in some ways, we are much like the seed and its growth process.

A seed is made of an embryo, that is, a baby plant that has all it needs to grow, develop, and blossom into what it was created to be. The embryo has the materials to develop its leaves, stems, and roots to gather needed nutriments from water, light, minerals, and such to produce food and provide support for itself. That's what we're like when we're born. We have all we need to be who we were created to be—all the unique qualities, talents and knowledge that is needed in the world.

✣ *The Seed and the Pod*

N OW THE SEED has another part that it needs for its growth, and that's its seed covering or pod. The pod provides protection, support, and nutrition to the seed during the growth process. It provides food for the seed until it can produce food on its own, and protects it from harsh elements in the environment. We also have something similar to the pod in our lives to help protect our seed from harm and support it during our growth process. We tend to look at the seed and pod in much like our true and false selves. The true or real self, like the seed, is the life-giving core of our being. The real self holds all the beauty and light of whom we are—it is the soul of the individual. The true self also has our entire real feelings and thoughts, feelings, and thoughts that may not be acceptable to those around us.

This is where the pod or our false self enters the scene. Like the pod, the false self protects and hides the real self from harsh elements of the environment. The false self responds to the demands, beliefs and possible abuse from our parents or caretakers, family, siblings, peers and other places and people that impact us as we grow. The false self takes on the mistaken beliefs, misguided directions, and sometimes harsh treatment we experience as we are growing up so our true self is never touched. The false self or pod becomes our mask, our facade to the outside world, to conceal and defend our true self, our little seed.

✣ *The Pod within Us*

T HE POD, AS we become older, begins to be written on by all the things we are told: all our experiences—bad and good—and all the wounds we gather throughout our life. Our pod may have written on it that we are worthless or bad or stupid. We may believe that we are good at certain things, but bad at other things like math or communication. We may think we should not show anger, fear, or pain to others. We may believe that people are not to be trusted or that confrontation is bad. There are many beliefs and ideas that our pod or false self takes in and learns from others. Some might not like the false self, because they think it keeps them from their seed. Actually, though, the pod has kept our seed safe until the time is right for the growth process. Once again, the seed's growth process can help us to understand our own growth process, our discovery of ourselves.

✣ *Preparing for Growth*

THE SEED WILL only grow and break through the pod when the environmental conditions are right, when there is just the right amount of warmth, moisture, and oxygen present around the seed. If the environment is too dry or has unfavorable temperatures, then the seed will not come out of its pod. This allows the plant to survive during periods when plant growth is not possible. It's the same for us! Our seed, our real self, is wise and does not allow itself to be in an environment that cannot support it or care for it. So, the seed waits until the time is right—until we are ready and able to have the support, internally and externally, for our seed to grow. This preparation time is very important so we can begin to let go of our pod with all inscribed beliefs and thoughts that do not belong to us and never did.

Some might say they have always been ready to let go of their pod. Yet, it takes honesty and courage to face what is in our pod and to see it is not who we truly are. This means we have to see that those who gave us these beliefs or hurt us were wrong. That is not to say these people were bad, for they learned these misguided ideas from their experiences, too, and they just didn't know any better. That's not always easy to accept about our parents, family, or loved ones. This growth process is not easy either. It takes much work, dedication, and willingness to look at some difficult issues.

✣ *A Story of Wheat and Weeds*

NOW, THE SEED can't just come out of its pod all at once, but it happens slowly at a gradual pace so that the growth is strong and sure. That means it's okay to allow elements of the pod to remain around the seed until you are ready to let go of those parts.

This process is like the story of a man who planted some wheat in his field. Then during the night, the man's enemy came and planted weeds among the wheat. When the wheat began to come up through the soil so did the weeds, and the man's servants asked him if they should gather up the weeds. The man replied, "No, because while you are gathering up the weeds, you might uproot the wheat with them. Rather, let both grow together. Then at harvest time, we will gather the weeds first, bind them together and burn them. Then we will gather the wheat into my barn."

In the meantime, if you have an issue written on your pod, like a hot temper or fear of confrontation, you can develop healthy and healing ways to deal with the issue. Then as one grows and discovers more about their seed, the elements in the pod will naturally fade.

⁜ Self-Discovery

IN THE PLANT'S growth process, first a root comes out of the pod to test the environment and the seed begins to build its root system to support the plant. Then the seed forms its leaves and stem to come up through the soil to the sunlight. That's what our seed does, too. First, our seed will build a foundation of who we truly are—our values, our ideas, our beliefs— to support our being and growth process. Then when the foundation is laid and our roots are firmly in the ground, we begin to break through the surface and our being begins to shine to the world. We discover who we truly are in just the right time and just the right way.

A good exercise to begin or further your awakening process is to write down on a piece of paper a list of all that is within your seed and what is written on your pod. You might want to draw and write about these qualities in depth. Look at where the elements of your pod came from, where you learned them, and what triggers these in you. You could also make a collage about your seed and pod using pictures, words, and sentences from magazines and newspapers to get a full picture of your growth process.

⁜ Everyone Is Unique

IT'S IMPORTANT TO recognize and appreciate our unique qualities. It takes effort and persistence to travel through this process, but remember your seed and pod have all they need to do the work. All that is required is already within you, and that's pretty amazing—just like the plant's little seed.

❧ *Appreciating Personality Diversity*

NOW THAT YOU understand your own personality better, take a look at those who work for you. Wouldn't it be great if everyone who worked for us had the exact same personalities that we do? No, it would not.

The most effective managers appreciate the diversity of their subordinates' personalities. That's the view of Management Professor Scott Williams, a business school faculty member at Wright State University in Dayton, Ohio.

"Personality diversity can make communication and coordination of activities more difficult at times, but diversity has its advantages," says Dr. Williams. "Diverse groups that give the extra effort to understand and accept each other's personalities tend to produce **higher quality decisions** than groups that are either (a) homogeneous or (b) don't manage their diversity well."

According to Dr. Williams, appreciating the diverse personalities of the people we interact with helps us to understand why they act the way they do and how to get the most out of them. Appreciating personality diversity means respecting the strengths and limitations of each individual, and knowing how to capitalize on each individual's strengths.

In his online newsletter *LeaderLetter*, Dr. Williams states that appreciating personality diversity is the opposite of dogmatically expecting everyone to view situations the way you do—no matter how successful you have been using your approach. We don't all think alike, but that's often a good thing.

"People with different personalities have different inherent strengths and weaknesses," adds Dr. Williams. "For this reason, the best groups are made up of members with diverse personalities who learn to appreciate and put to use each other's strengths. Managers should promote an appreciation for personality diversity. Discussions of personality inventories, especially when facilitated by an expert, can be an effective way to foster such appreciation."

7

%% Helping Employees with Career Transitions

Applying Personality Assessment Psychology

THIS IS THE story of two employees at two different companies. Let's call them Bob and Marcia. Both had been loyal, hardworking employees, but it was decided the fit just wasn't right. Bob was told by email and then escorted out of the building by security. Marcia was told in a face-to-face discussion by her manager who also knew Marcia's personality traits. Together they worked out a career transition plan. Bob is suing his company. Marcia has moved on but has good things to say about her former employer.

What is the difference in these two scenarios? In one instance, company actions triggered Bob's anger and catapulted him down the legal pathway. In the other, Marcia's bosses were aware that termination is an emotional issue and should be managed.

Many managers, when faced with the challenge of firing someone, forget, avoid, or are unaware of the emotions that are experienced by the person being fired. Experts say that the death of a loved one, a divorce or long-term relationship breakup, and the loss of one's job have an equal and similar impact on one's emotions. Think for a moment about the loss of one of your dear relatives or friends through death. How did you feel? That's exactly the same feeling that people have when they suddenly and unexpectedly lose their jobs.

One company owner we know of had a unique way of transitioning people out of the company. He never had a legal problem either. When he brought in someone to let them go, he told them that it isn't working here but there is someplace that would be right for them. He offered to work on that together with them. He asked them to gather their things that day and leave, and then call him tomorrow or the next day and they would work together to find a place that would be right for them. Few took him up on the offer, but all appreciated that he was on their side.

In her 1969 book, *On Death and Dying*, Swiss-born psychiatrist Elizabeth Kübler-Ross outlined the five stages of grief of someone who is dying. Kübler-Ross originally applied these stages to any form of catastrophic personal loss, including a job and income. This also includes the death of a loved one and divorce. The **Kübler-Ross model** describes, in five discrete stages, the process by which people deal with grief and tragedy. Terminally ill patients are said to experience these stages. The stages have become well-known, and are called the *Five Stages of Grief*. The stages are:

1. **Denial**: The initial stage: *"It can't be happening."*

2. **Anger**: *"Why me? It's not fair?!"* (either referring to God, oneself, or anybody perceived, rightly or wrongly, as "responsible")

3. **Bargaining**: *"Just let me hang on until after the holidays."*

4. **Depression**: *"I'm so sad, why bother with anything?"*

5. **Acceptance**: *"It's going to be okay."*

Kübler-Ross also claimed these steps do not necessarily come in order, nor are they all experienced by all individuals, though she stated a person will always experience at least two.

It is vitally important to realize that all people will go through the five stages of the grief cycle (quite often at different paces) and as a manager, it is your responsibility to help them progress through these stages, particularly the first two that are likely to occur when they are still with the company.

❧ *Helping Your Employees with Emotions during Career Transitions*

THE FOLLOWING CHECKLIST is adapted from Bob Selden, who has been a supervisor, manager and senior manager in a number of both large and small organizations. During his career, he has had to grapple with the challenges of hiring and firing. Now, as managing director of the National Learning Institute in Australia, he offers his advice free to managers and aspiring managers on how to best supervise their people.

> ➤ Before taking any action, review the person's personality assessment and ask yourself: Based on the personality profile, how would I feel if I were this person and my boss came to me today and said, 'You're fired!' Write down a list of words that describe your feelings.

> ➤ Based on your personality assessment, if you were in the situation of being fired, how would you like your boss to handle it? What would you like him/her to do and to say? Jot down some of your thoughts.

> ➤ Now write down a list of the words that best describe your feelings about having to fire someone. Review all the words you have scribbled down so far and pick out the two or three strongest. Also keep in mind how you would like to be handled in similar circumstances.

> ➤ Based on your knowledge of the personality traits involved, script the start of the conversation using the two or three words you have discovered. For example, "This is really difficult for me. I feel apprehensive and worried that I won't get it right."

> ➤ The next part of your opening script will depend on the circumstances. For example in a lay-off situation, it might go something like: "I have been advised that I have to terminate the employment of a number of people. I am really sad to say that your name is on that list." Or, for a non-performance issue, it could be something like: "We have discussed my expectations about your performance and unfortunately they are still not being met. It now really saddens me [or whatever your feelings are] that I will have to terminate your employment."

➤ Be careful. You can only script the opening few lines, but they are important because they set the scene for the entire interview.

➤ It is most likely that during the remainder of the interview, the employee will travel backward and forwards between shock and resistance. Give your reasons for the termination clearly and succinctly, but do not get into a discussion about justifying yours (or your employer's) reasons. Doing so will keep the employee fixed in either of the first two stages and will not help them to progress. Only sincere listening and clear questioning (not reasoning) will help the employee progress to the acceptance stage.

According to Selden, one factor that is often overlooked when firing someone is that the way it is done can have as much impact (positive or negative) on the people who remain. They will be watching (and will invariably get a firsthand report from their colleague) about how well or otherwise the process was managed. The people who remain in the organization, and whom I assume you want to keep, get a good look at both the manager's and the organization's real people management skills when under the stress of firing someone. They will most certainly ask, "Could this happen to me?"

✦ *How to Help with Transitions*

WHETHER ONE HAS been in a career for many years or just beginning, career switches are not easy to navigate. It can be very difficult to find the career path that is right. Here is how you can advise your employees when you are helping them to make a transition (and of course, this advice will be helpful if you are the one who needs to make the job switch).

Sometimes we may find ourselves trying to live up to someone else's expectations rather than our own, or we don't know what we want in a career—what will make us happy.

So, where does one start in a career search? First, don't panic, as that will be picked up when applying for positions. Yet, don't deny the feelings of anger, hurt and fear either. A good way to deal with these feelings is to talk to a counselor, clergy person, or friend, and journal out your feelings. That will help to resolve the feelings so they don't get in the way of your career search.

⚜ *Finding Your Direction*

INDING THE RIGHT career can be a very confusing and scary process. So, what are some small steps to find that career path? Here's an exercise that you might find helpful in making an action plan for your career search.

First, dream about three things you'd love to do in life. What turns you on? What gets your blood going? Some examples could be going to the moon, being a Broadway star, or exploring ancient ruins. Don't put limits on your dreams—write them all down. This will help you to discover in what pathways you are most interested.

What is it about these three ideas that excites you? Let's use the example of going to the moon. It may be the instruments in the Space Shuttle that excite you. Focus in on what is so interesting about your dreams.

What is it about the (you fill in the blank) in your dreams that excites you? What is it about those Space Shuttle instruments that you find interesting?

Now, you get to research. So, go to the library, Internet, college career placement centers, or other resources to research the companies associated with what excites you. With the Space Shuttle example, you might research the manufacturers of the Space Shuttle.

Then contact a company representative in the department that interests you the most. You may be interested in design, sales, marketing, accounting, etc., so ask for that department when calling. Emphasize that you are doing research when calling, as people seem to be more helpful. You'll gain information on opportunities and job requirements in the company and the industry. Also, ask what other companies or contacts would be helpful in your research. This can give you possible referrals and assist with networking. As part of your research, see if you can visit the area where you want to work and talk to people who are in your desired career field. This will help you decide if this is the right career for you.

Sometimes, we can be too close to the situation and need help to find our way. When this is the case, be sure to reach out for assistance from a counselor, clergy person, and friends. Support is very important during this difficult process.

⚜ *Researching Is the Key*

R ESEARCH IS A very important part in any career search, whether it is to find that perfect career or new position. Many people do very little research or preparation in their search, a practice that failed us in school and will fail us in our job search. How many people do you know who obtained a graduate degree only to discover to their horror that they hate their new career? If you want that great career or position, be sure you are ready in all ways for it!

When coauthor Ellen graduated from college, she didn't know what she wanted to do. So, she thought about what she liked and researched three areas—business, computers and psychology. She gathered information on different careers and companies in these three areas by looking in the library's reference section and contacting companies, individuals, and counselors. She asked about the job requirements, pros and cons, and the daily routine of the desired careers. At the time, she used this information to obtain a business position in a corporation then later made a career change to counseling. This process helped her to decide what pathway was right for her at that time in her life.

⚜ *Effective Interviewing Tips*

S o, NOW THAT we have a direction to go in, how do we prepare for our career search? Here are some interviewing tips to help you on your way.

➢ Be sure to research the company and position fully before the interview. Know the salary range ahead of time and how long the previous employee had been in the position. Knowing how long employees have been in the position will help key you in to any danger signs. It can signal whether this opportunity is the door to heaven or hell.

➢ Self-image is very important in interviewing. Make sure your suit or interviewing outfit is in good shape and pressed. Keep appearances fairly conservative, like neat hair, no long fingernails and light on perfume/cologne and jewelry. This advice may bother some, but appearances are vital in interviewing. As you may know, an interviewer usually makes a decision within the first ten minutes after meeting the interviewee. It's important to put your best foot forward, so the interviewer can focus on you and your thought process.

➤ Successful resumes and cover letters target the position. Go to the library or bookstore to get ideas for effective resumes and cover letters. Keep resumes and cover letters brief and to the point—one page in length, and targeted to the desired position. Be sure to cover all areas of job requirements from the job listing in the cover letter. For example, if the listing calls for five years of experience with gadgets then put that in the cover letter. Or if you don't have that experience, be sure to address it with similar experience or skills. Also, different jobs call for different resumes, like a sales resume for a sales job or a management resume for a management job. There is a different emphasis for each job type. Plus, you always need an original cover letter for each position. Don't use form letters, as they are too general and unfocused. After the interview, always send a thank you note. It gives you the edge over others who don't. It's also important to have someone else proof your resume, cover letters, and thank you letters to watch for grammar and spelling errors.

➤ Practice makes perfect! Before the interview, practice with interview questions. You can get sample questions from career books at the library. If possible, practice with a friend. Role play the whole interview from handshake to good-byes. You can even video the interview to study how to improve your interviewing style. Be prepared to discuss your strengths and weaknesses; what you liked and disliked about your last position (in a positive manner—don't complain about supervisors); and why the company should hire you. Keep your answers brief and to the point, using workplace examples in a positive manner. Be able to discuss difficult areas like employment gaps or lack of experience. Remember that this is the time to toot your own horn. If you don't believe in yourself, then it will be hard for an employer to believe in you.

➤ Be prepared for that big interview. Take an extra resume copy to the interview and fill out all forms completely. Confirm your interview before going. Always ask one question about the company—something you want to know—but avoid asking about salary and benefits in the first interview. Ask for business cards to send thank you notes after the interview.

➤ You make the decision. Look around the company environment to be sure you feel comfortable there. The interview process is not a one-way procedure. You have to decide if this is the right place for you. So, look at everything and everyone at the company to help you make the right decision. Listen to your intuition. If it feels wrong, then it's probably not the right place for you.

➤ Assess the interview for self-improvement. What could you do differently? Yet, don't beat yourself up for nervous slip-ups. We're all human, and we all make mistakes.

⬥ *There's a Place for Everyone*

FINALLY, WE WANT to leave you with a story to ponder. A friend once told us about a young lady who was trying to sell her car to pay her college tuition. She was having little luck and tuition was due in a few days. She drove her car into a gas station and began to cry in frustration.

The owner of the gas station came over to see what was wrong, and she told him her tale of woe. When she was finished with her story, he made an interesting, if somewhat inspiring reply. He said, "Honey, let me tell you something. There's an ass for every seat!" Then he suggested she leave her car at the gas station, and he'd see what he could do.

The next day the car was sold, and the young lady was able to pay her tuition. The owner would not even take a commission for the sale. When life seems dark and hopeless, this story can remind us that everyone has a perfect place in life. So, no matter how tough things may be, the right pathway is waiting for all of us. The key is to maintain our vision.

8

⁄⁄ How to Manage Difficult People

Handling the Difficult without Difficulty

A s a manager, you must deal with a wide range of personalities. Thanks to proper hiring assessments, most of your direct reports should be productive and reasonable workers. But what about those who slip through the process, employees you inherit, or co-workers who are extremely difficult to work with or even be around? You know the types. These are the folks focused on their own agenda and needs, who cause conflicts wherever they go, and command a great deal of a manager's time and attention. The difficult ones don't get diseases like ulcers and heart attacks. They seem to induce them in others!

During our workshops on managing difficult people, we always express a debt of gratitude to a pair of doctors named Rick: Rick Brinkman and Rick Kirschner, authors of two great reads, *Dealing with People You Can't Stand* and their latest, *Dealing with Difficult People*. They became friends while med-students, but their friendship blossomed when a surgeon from an area hospital became their mentor. With his guidance and encouragement, they studied health from an attitudinal point of view. In 1982, a mental-health organization asked the two Ricks to create a program on how to deal with difficult people. That marked the official beginning of a research project that has continued for more than twenty-five years.

Another author who is an important voice on this subject is psychologist Jay Carter, whose book *Nasty People* calls upon decades of practice and observation to offer proven strategies for avoiding toxic relationships (www.jaycarter.net). With psychology that makes sense, Dr. Carter offers tremendous insights on how to protect your sanity and confront emotional bullies. The process begins by identifying the "invalidators" in your work life. (The following excerpts are used with permission of the author and the McGraw-Hill Companies, publishers of *Nasty People* by Dr. Jay Carter, copyright 2003—second edition.)

⚜ *Taking on Invalidation*

IN THE WORDS of Leo Buscaglia, "Only the weak are cruel. Gentleness can only be expected from the strong." Have you been hurt, betrayed, or degraded by a difficult employee, co-worker, or boss? Whoever that person is, according to Dr. Carter, he or she is an invalidator who feeds upon your self-esteem, mental anguish, and unhappiness. But you can stop this cycle of abuse and put an end to sneak attacks, without stooping to their level.

"Invalidation is a general term for a person injuring or trying to injure another," says Dr. Carter. "An invalidation can range anywhere from a shot in the back to a 'tsk, tsk.' A rolling of the eyeballs can be an invalidation and so can a punch in the nose. It is usually the sneaky verbal or non-verbal invalidations that cause the most damage. A punch in the nose is obvious, and it heals. However, an attack on self esteem ... at the right moment ... and in the right way ... can last a lifetime."

The major reason invalidation occurs so often in the workplace is that it seems to work. The sneaky invalidation works because a punch in the nose is obvious and will get the troublemaker terminated (if not sued), while the mental attack may go unnoticed and unpunished, while it injures its victim.

According to Dr. Carter, invalidation is propagated in our society by about 20 percent of the population. "About 1 percent intentionally spread this misery, while the other 19 percent do it unconsciously. Invalidation can be found to greater and lesser degrees in various societies. Happier individuals evolve from societies in which invalidation is at a minimum. Unfortunately, in the US, it seems to be part of the American way."

For a manager it may be problematic to identify invalidation, as the methods used to invalidate are often very subtle. When people invalidate, it is because they feel inferior to others. To compensate, they attack and undermine the self-esteem of others. Invalidating behavior ranges from very obvious to covert.

Where does invalidation come from? People express invalidating behavior either consciously or subconsciously. Most people slip into this behavior subconsciously by reacting to subtle triggers in the environment and have learned this from others, like a family member. This behavior is passed from one person to another through being invalidated.

⚜ *Common Methods of Invalidation*

FOREWARNED IS FOREARMED, as the old adage goes. Be on the watch for these low blows and cheap shots.

Building You Up, Cutting You Down
When an individual showers you with compliments, then tears you apart.

Cutting You Off
When someone cuts off communication in the middle. He or she may ask you a question, then cuts you off or walks off before you are finished answering.

Projection
A psychological mechanism, where the individual takes his/her own feelings and puts the responsibility for them onto someone else, as if these feelings originated within the other person.

Generalization
When a person uses generalizations that are simply exaggerations of small truths. The more truth there is in the generalization, the more it can be exaggerated. "Always" and "never" are commonly used in generalizations.

Double Message
This method uses opposite messages to confuse and put down the other person.

The Double Bind
When you are set up in a situation where you are "damned if you do and damned if you don't."

⟐ How to Handle Invalidation

WHEN YOU RECOGNIZE the tactics of the difficult people, then you can have a counter strategy. Here are a few tips and techniques to counter their assaults.

"Just the Facts"
Sticking to and firmly repeating the facts is a powerful way to destroy invalidation.

"What Did You Say?"
Asking the person to repeat the invalidation will, at times, defuse it, especially if it was a sneak attack.

Tell It Like It Is
Most invalidations are insinuations, voice inflections, and double messages that can be handled with the simple truth. Tell the truth by looking at your feelings. "I feel angry when you speak to me in that manner."

Don't Let It Slide
Invalidation only gets worse as time goes on. It's important to talk about it. Exploring the intent is helpful to reduce invalidation, by asking, "When you say that, what are you really trying to say?"

Maintain Boundaries
Saying no, putting down limits, and describing what you can do is helpful when dealing with someone who is using pressure, demands, or manipulation to get what they want.

❧ *Five Other Types of Difficult Behavior*

INVALIDATORS ARE NOT the only challenge for a manager. At best, the following types of difficult behavior make work life tense, stressful and unpleasant. At worst, they can keep a manager from achieving important goals. We all know what happens to managers who don't achieve their goals. But through knowledge and practice, you can obtain the power to bring out the best behavior in direct reports and co-workers who are at their worst.

According to Drs. Brinkman and Kirschner, there are many different types of difficult behavior at work, and behavior can change from one type to another as conditions change. You have the advantage when you are prepared with a variety of responses when dealing with any particular difficult behavior. Here are five types of difficult behavior and suggestions on how to deal with them. (The following excerpts are used with permission of the authors and the McGraw-Hill Companies, publishers of *Dealing With Difficult People: 24 Lessons for Bringing Out the Best in Everyone* by Dr. Rick Brinkman and Dr. Rick Kirschner, copyright 2003—first edition.)

⫸ *The Authority: "I know it all"*

APERSON BEHAVING THIS way has a low tolerance for correction or contradiction, and easily blames others when things go wrong. According to Brinkman and Kirschner, here is your goal: To open their mind to new ideas and information.

How to handle them:

1. Be prepared and know the flaws and shortcomings of your ideas. Be able to explain them in a brief, precise, and clear manner.

2. Use active listening to help the person know you are listening to them, and be sure to show interest and respect.

3. Acknowledge and address the problems and doubts, by paraphrasing the concern back with information to address it.

4. Present your ideas indirectly by using softening words (like, "perhaps," "what do you suppose") to sound hypothetical rather than challenging. Use plural pronouns like "we" or "us" to convey that you are both on the same team. Ask questions to help the individual to accept new information, like, "I was wondering, what do you suppose would happen if we were to try [new information] in certain areas?"

5. Use them as resources by letting them know that you recognize them as an expert and are willing to learn from them. They will spend more time teaching you than obstructing you.

⚱ *The Fake: "Look at me!"*

FAKING INVOLVES ACTING or pretending that we're something we're not for approval, attention and/or importance. In the business world, this behavior can be especially destructive when people act as experts and give out misinformation and opinions as facts.

People behaving this way combine a small amount of information with exaggeration and generalizations to get attention. When confronted, these individuals can get very aggressive to maintain their facade. This is driven by a strong people focus since people are the source of the attention and appreciation they crave.

Here are some recommendations on how to handle them:

1. Give them a little attention by:

   ➢ Repeating back their comments with enthusiasm.

   ➢ Acknowledging their positive intent rather than wasting time debating their content. Example: "Thanks for contributing to this discussion."

   ➢ You don't have to agree with their remarks to provide some attention or positive projection.

2. Ask some revealing questions to clarify for specifics. Fakes usually talk in generalizations, so ask questions to get specifics. For example, when they use "always," ask "when specifically?" Ask your questions with curiosity and respect, and not to embarrass the individual.

3. Tell it like it is and redirect the conversation back to reality and facts. Speak about the situation or problem from your point of view and use "I" statements to keep your remarks as non-threatening as possible.

4. Give them a break to reduce the chance of them becoming defensive. When providing evidence, you can say, "But maybe you haven't heard of this yet..." You can also act as if their misinformation has reminded you of your subject and express appreciation for their efforts.

5. Notice when the individual is doing something right and give credit where credit is due.

〰 *The No Person: "No! No! No!!!"*

T HE "NO PERSON" constantly says no to everything and strives to defeat ideas and fights for despair and hopelessness. (This person is the close cousin of the "no, but" person.)

Kirschner and Brinkman advise that you handle them like this:

1. Go with the flow. Allow the individual to be as negative as they want to be. Don't try to convince them that things are not so bad. That will only motivate them to convince you that things are even worse.

2. Use them as a detector for potential problems and discovering fatal flaws in a project or situation.

3. Give them time. "No people" tend to operate in a different time reality than other people. The more you push them to make a decision, the more they will dig in their heels.

4. Be realistic by acknowledging the flaws or problems, and invite them to help you in finding a solution.

5. Acknowledge their positive intent by acting as if the negative feedback is meant to be helpful. Appreciate them for having high standards, being willing to speak up, and being concerned about details. When a successful project is completed, remember to include them in the celebration.

⚜ *The Whiner: "Oh, woe is me!"*

THIS PERSON FEELS helpless and overwhelmed by an unfair world. They set their standard at perfection and nothing measures up to it. They constantly complain about everything and search out an audience to listen to their tale of woe.

Kirschner and Brinkman offer these suggestions for dealing with whiners:

1. <u>Do's and Don'ts</u>:

   ➢ Don't agree with them. That just encourages them to continue complaining.

   ➢ Don't disagree with them, as they'll feel the need to repeat their woes.

   ➢ Don't try to solve their problems—you can't.

   ➢ Do have patience with their unrealistic standards and endless negativity.

   ➢ Do have compassion for them as their lives seem to be beyond their control.

   ➢ Do have commitment to the process of getting them to focus on solutions.

2. Listen for and write down the main points in their complaints. This helps you to clarify the situation to prepare for the last step of this process.

3. Interrupt and be specific by asking clarification questions.

4. Whiners often complain in cascading generalizations and don't stand still with any one problem long enough to even start problem solving. It's important to stop them and get specific.

5. Shift the focus to solutions. As you get specific about each complaint, ask them, "What do you want?" They may not know, in which case tell them to make something up. Or if they do know, what is it?

6. Others may be unrealistic in their solutions, so help them be more practical by telling them like it is and saying, "Based on these facts, what do you want?"

7. Involve them in the problem solving process by having them track and document the problem in writing, and request solutions and recommendations for the problem. This helps them to see that problems can be solved.

8. If these steps have not created even a minor change with the individual, then you must politely but firmly draw the line. To draw the line:

> ➢ Each time the person begins to complain, you must take charge of the situation and bring it assertively to a close, by standing up and walking to the door.

> ➢ Say calmly, "Since your complaints seem to have no solutions, talking about them isn't going to accomplish anything. If you happen to think of any solutions, please let me know."

> ➢ Do not allow them to draw you back into their cycle of complaining. Simply repeat the same statement over and over.

⟐ *The Yes Person: "I just can't say no!"*

THIS INDIVIDUAL CONSTANTLY tries to please others and avoid confrontation by saying yes to everyone. They have trouble thinking things through and consistently overextend themselves. They react to the latest requests and demands, fail to follow through, and end up feeling resentful towards others.

Kirschner and Brinkman offer these suggestions on how to handle them:

1. Make it safe to discuss anger and fear in a calm manner. The key to maintaining safety is using active listening and verbal reassurance.

2. Talk honestly without getting defensive. Ask them questions to clarify and express your appreciation for their honesty, like, "Please help me to understand what happened last week. What stopped you from having the information on time? Did you ask anyone for help?"

3. Help them learn to plan. This is an opportunity to change and learn how to keep commitments.

   ➢ Start with stating the consequence of breaking one's promises. Example: "One of the most important parts of being a team is knowing that my team can count on me and I can count on my team. Just think how it would affect our ability to be a team and work together if we couldn't keep our commitments to each other."

   ➢ Help them to look at different options and make changes. Ask questions like, "What got in the way and what could have been done differently? How else could the situation have been handled?" Example: "Instead of saying yes right away when someone asks you to do something, perhaps you can train yourself to say, 'Let me look at my schedule and get back to you.'"

   ➢ Help the individual focus on specific action steps to accomplish the task.

4. Ensure commitment by:

   ➢ Seeking a deeper level of commitment by asking for their "word of honor."

- Asking them to summarize their commitment by having them tell you what they will do. Example: "I want to make sure that you and I both understand how this will be done. Could you describe to me what you will do and when?"

- Having them write it down, which will make the information easier to remember.

- Being very clear about the deadlines and describing negative consequences in terms of how a broken commitment will affect others. Example: "If this doesn't get completed, how do you think that is going to impact those who are depending on you?"

- Keeping in touch to help the person overcome any obstacles and ensure follow through.

5. Strengthen the relationship by acknowledging when the individual is honest about their doubts and concerns; dealing with broken promises with great care; and making an event out of every completed commitment.

How to deal with broken promises:

- Tell them what they did by specifically describing the facts of the situation, but not your opinion of the situation. Example: "You made a commitment to finish this project."

- Explain how others were affected in a factual manner. Tell them how you feel about it. Don't exaggerate, but be honest. Example: "Quite honestly, I'm disappointed and frustrated over this."

- Project positive intent, like, "I know you care about doing great work and you are capable of doing what you say."

- Tell them, "That's not like you," even if it is. People will strive to fulfill positive projections.

- Ask them what they learned from the experience and how they would handle it differently. This helps to change negative situations into learning experiences.

⁜ *You Are in Control of You*

MANAGERS ARE INFLUENTIAL, but the only person you can control is you. So keep a positive attitude about dealing with negative people. As Betty Sachelli put it, "Two thoughts cannot occupy the mind at the same time, so the choice is ours as to whether our thoughts will be constructive or destructive."

Difficult employees are a fact of life. They blame, intimidate, whine, run away, or explode without notice. The more you try to work with them, the more they seem to work to disrupt your plans. But there's no reason to let difficult employees get in the way of your performance in the workplace. With the help of these effective approaches to understanding and circumventing disruptive and annoying behavior, you can get past the roadblocks posed by difficult people in the workplace.

9

%%% From Managing to Leading

How to Become a Vision-Focused Leader

Now that you have cracked the personality code and are hiring and managing better, what's next?

The answer is leadership. It is time to become a vision-focused leader around whom issues can be raised and resolved productively. That's the view of Suzanne and Dwight Frindt, the founders of 2130 Partners, a leadership development and education firm that facilitates focused vision, inspired teams, and sustained commitment for its clients.

Ask yourself these questions:

➢ Are your conversations with your team generating the results you want?

➢ Does your team successfully raise and resolve issues relevant to business success?

➢ Can you identify and deal with emotional upsets, in both yourself and others?

Exactly what is this leadership that is vision-focused? "We love Warren Bennis' definition: 'Leadership is the wise use of power. Power is the capacity to translate intention into reality and sustain it,'" says Suzanne Frindt. "Our approach is the same whether we are working with individuals or with entire leadership teams. We believe the greatest opportunities are created by the development of people and action in a coordinated direction. We assert that the only sustainable strategies engage the heart and soul and are simultaneously grounded in sound business practices."

Suzanne Frindt co-founded 2130 Partners with her husband Dwight in 1990. She is a recognized speaker on the topics of Vision-Focused Leadership™ and Productive Interactions™ (www.2130partners.com), speaking to various organizations around the world. Suzanne is also a group chair for Vistage International, Inc., an organization dedicated to increasing the effectiveness and enhancing the lives of more than 14,000 CEO and executive members in sixteen countries.

Dwight Frindt established 2130 Partners on an idea that has become the cornerstone of the firm. The guiding methodology of Vision-Focused Leadership was born from his years of hands-on executive experience and from his thirty-year affiliation with The Hunger Project, an organization committed to the sustainable end of world hunger. Dwight has integrated his knowledge of managing operations, acquisitions, and turn-arounds with insights he has learned through the work of The Hunger Project in rural villages around the world. Dwight also serves as a group chair for Vistage International and monthly facilitates CEO and executive groups in Orange County, California.

In their leadership programs, through their firm 2130 Partners, the Frindts train participants to utilize a new paradigm and methodology to shift the way they listen and dialogue. This critical approach enhances fundamental skills and abilities to have successful interactions—the cornerstone of effective leadership.

⚜ *Power of Shared Vision*

IN A **1996** article in the *Harvard Business Review* entitled "Building Your Company's Vision," Jim Collins and Jerry Porras said that companies that enjoy enduring success have a core purpose and core values that remain fixed while their strategies and practices endlessly adapt to a changing world. The rare ability to balance continuity and change—requiring a consciously practiced discipline—is closely linked to the ability to develop a vision.

Vision provides guidance about what to preserve and what to change. Suzanne Frindt calls vision a "Yonder Star."

"Without a vision, what is the point?" says Suzanne Frindt. "A Yonder Star unleashes the energy to galvanize yourself and your employees so you can achieve phenomenal things."

When group members share a vision, it creates an opportunity for totally different conversations between a manager and members of their team. Focus on the shared vision creates alignment and provides a powerful context for creating mission, strategic initiatives, objectives, goals, roles, and finally all the way down through action plans.

Being a manager means making choices. At any moment in time you have a decision to make. Suzanne urges that when it comes time to make a decision being present in the moment, not on automatic pilot, is essential to the quality and relevance of the decision. You can then make the choice based on your Yonder Star, your shared vision of something to which you aspire, versus more of the same or your fear of some worst-case scenario.

"Worries are about envisioning a worst-case scenario, what you fear most," says Suzanne Frindt. "Whatever we envision is affecting us right now. What we envision impacts us in this moment. There are consequences for managing based on fears that you may not want. Your Yonder Star is the shared vision you aspire to. The star is what you envision, and what you envision shapes both the present moment and the quality of your choices about your actions."

Something else she recommends avoiding is being past-focused. This is when you make decisions based solely on what you have done in the past. Instead of having an inspiring vision for your team, all you are working for with a past based focus is attempting to minimize perceived risk and making incremental improvements.

"Many companies are past-focused when they do strategic planning," says Suzanne Frindt. "What did the company do last year and then let's add 10 percent or 20 percent. We are all tempted to try hard to make yesterday look like today. Or if we didn't like yesterday, then we try to make it different or better."

She adds that only by having a vision, a Yonder Star, can teams create breakthroughs to unprecedented results. Equally important is that it is a shared vision, one that is based on shared values and shared operating principles. This is how you create an environment for real collaboration.

The Frindts also advise their clients to learn to shift from being monologuers to dialoguers. As Margaret Miller once said, "Most conversations are simply monologues delivered in the presence of witnesses." A monologuer manager is driven by proving they are right rather than engaging in a conversation for creative problem solving. This monologuing manager often gets surrender and appeasement from their team members rather than enthusiastic engagement.

Dialogue is the opposite. The three Cs of dialoguing are connect, converse and create. It has been said that the purpose of dialogue is not to share information but to create information. The focus is on the issue and your shared purpose rather than each other. As a manager, your ability to model and encourage listening that is curious and open dramatically increases your effectiveness. The dimensions that become possible are creativity, connection, alignment, focus, and collaboration.

"You create your vision, honestly assess where you are, and then get to work on the gap," says Suzanne Frindt. "On the road there will be roadblocks and potholes. As a manager you work with your team to get around the roadblocks and fill in potholes."

⚜ *Overcoming Emotional Barriers*

"THE ABILITY TO identify and clear upsets, in myself and others, is the single most significant key to productivity gains in our economy today," says Dwight Frindt. "We have asked our executive-leadership clients a simple question: 'What time could you go home if everyone in the company simply came to work, did their jobs, and went home?' The answer used to surprise us until it kept being repeated. On average, our clients say, 'Between 10:30 a.m. and 11:00 a.m.'"

That begs a second question. If so many executives claim they could go home before lunch if everyone just showed up and did their work, what's taking so much of our leaders' time? The Frindts' clients tell them flat out: distress, commonly known as upsets. The most time-consuming part of their job is managing the distressed interactions within their teams so that those teams can actually get to the business at hand.

"Okay, let's assume there's gross exaggeration at play here, fueled by frustration and wry humor," continues Dwight Frindt. "But even if executives will never be able to consistently leave by noon, it is entirely reasonable for them to expect to save at least two hours of their time, every day. Alternatively they could increase their productivity 15–30%"

That's nearly 500 extra hours a year leaders can devote to creative thinking, visioning, and strategizing rather than on repairing relationships and soothing bruised egos. At the opportunity cost of most executives' time, that amounts to very substantial savings. Of course, the same can be said for everyone in the organization. An inordinate amount of productive time and payroll dollars and worse yet, opportunities, are lost daily, monthly and annually to the distraction caused by unresolved emotional distress.

Replacing that time, energy, and resource loss is of paramount importance. Doing so can create a culture that is both highly productive and emotionally resilient and rewarding. It requires a fundamental, transformative shift in two steps: 1) fewer emotionally driven issues in the workplace; and 2) leaders and their team members becoming self-sufficient in handling emotional distress issues when they occur.

"Let's clarify what we mean by emotional distress," says Dwight Frindt. "We're using the term to summarize a wide range of reactions that temporarily disable people with regard to thoughtful and productive behavior. These reactions can vary from mild frustration to full-blown anger, and include embarrassment, sadness, impatience, agitation, worry, and fear. In each case the person is left in a condition where, whether realized or not, they are acting as if their very survival is threatened."

⚛ The Causes of Emotional Distress

THE FRINDTS' STUDIES and their clients' experiences make it clear that the most common root causes of workplace emotional distress are 1) the perception that a promise has been broken (usually by leadership); 2) when positive intentions "fail"; and 3) when commitments seem thwarted. In addition to these three internal triggers, there are many times when personal distress is brought to the workplace from the rest of the person's life. These other sources can be especially difficult to address, due to varying perspectives on what constitutes personal-professional boundaries.

The impact on the productivity and organizational effectiveness of people attempting to work while "stressed out" (or surrounded by others who are) is enormous. Yet it's been the Frindts' observation that most leaders overlook this as the place to start any efforts in business improvement. Most are far more comfortable with cost cutting, process development, process improvement, reorganizing, or some other business change that does not directly address the human dimension.

To help disarm this apparent reluctance to actively engage when emotional distress is present, the Frindts began several years ago to bring their clients a variety of expert presentations, books, and other training opportunities for building communication and issue-resolution skills. Even though there are many excellent resources available in this field, they were disappointed in the results. Their clients' progress after exposure to all this material fell significantly short of what had been anticipated. The clients' ability and skill in powerfully addressing emotional, distressing situations didn't dramatically change.

So what went wrong? Why didn't all that training and exposure to skill-building help when emotional distress was triggered? The problem is not in the content of the material. It's in the limitation of its focus. Most of this highly regarded material addresses and is received by the intellectual part of the mind. That's fine, as far as it goes, but too often the audience comes away with a conceptual understanding while gaining little or no real skill at changing behavior. Providing access to new information and a broader intellectual understanding is a good start, but it's only a start. The Frindts found that unless this information is somehow deeply absorbed and embodied beyond the intellect, it vanishes when people are challenged and faced with intense emotion—their own or that of others.

⚜ *Understanding the Role of Your Body*

STUDIES HAVE SHOWN that to learn a new physical skill takes 300 repetitions for muscle-memory to be developed and 3,000 repetitions for the skill to be "embodied." In a similar way, the Frindts believe that for intellectual learning to take root, it must be practiced repeatedly. In addition, there are key physical components that impact intellectual learning, especially when someone is faced with stress.

Without awareness of these physical components, it's almost impossible to learn to address distress differently. The Frindts are finding that the physical aspects of being in an emotionally distressed state are as important as the feelings themselves. These two elements are inextricably linked. Ignoring or overlooking the physical manifestations of emotion limits our ability to manage emotional distress.

Research into brain physiology is now giving us valuable understanding of the physiological dimension of our emotional reactions. This fundamental information is extremely useful for business leaders. For example, let's look at a physical process sometimes referred to as "limbic hijacking."

The limbic system is the part of the brain associated with emotion and memory. Within the limbic system are the amygdalae, two almond-shaped clusters of neurons whose primary responsibilities include scanning for danger and warning us of impending threats. A limbic hijacking occurs when the amygdalae are triggered, producing physical sensations of distress. Some common signals of the amygdalae's work include sweaty palms, tense shoulders, dry mouth, and "butterflies in the stomach." As the intensity of distress rises, the strength of the physical signals increases—and our rational, cognitive powers diminish.

⚜ *A Biological Early Warning System*

IN THEIR ROLE as instinctual guardians, the amygdalae are part of our biological early warning system. They help ensure our physical survival by triggering four simple reactions: fight, flight, freeze, or appease. They respond instinctively, with lightning speed—much faster than the thinking portions of our brain.

For our early ancestors, who were dealing with a natural world that presented many real, life-threatening dangers, this function was essential to survival. But in today's corporate workplace, amygdalae reactions can often hinder instead of help.

Here's why. The amygdalae react instinctively, nearly instantaneously. Unfortunately, they can't differentiate between a real or imagined threat. They also can't distinguish between a physical threat and one generated by words or our own thoughts. And when the amygdalae send their warnings, they set powerful forces in motion throughout the body. Adrenaline and cortisol are released, raising heart rate and blood pressure. Blood drains from "less important" areas (such as our thinking brain) and goes to those areas needed for physical defense. We become a reactionary machine: on guard, on edge.

"Not the best state for thoughtful discourse, creative problem-solving or associative collaboration," notes Dwight Frindt.

⚹ *Post-Stress Mess*

THAT'S JUST THE beginning. There are also the after-effects. If we were running from a bear in the woods like our ancestors, that extreme physical effort would consume much of the excess adrenaline and cortisol released by the amygdalae's warnings of danger. Because of that, soon after the danger had passed, our heart rate and blood pressure would drop, and we would return to a more relaxed, thoughtful state.

In the office, this doesn't happen. On a typical working day the amygdalae may perceive many "threatening" situations. And even though these "dangers" take the form of spoken words or private thoughts rather than outside physical threats to our survival, they still trigger the same biological reactions. We get hyped up in self-defense mode with nowhere to run off the floods of adrenaline and cortisol.

Without a release, our heart rate and blood pressure stay high, other physical sensations continue, and we experience protracted stress. At a minimum, we're frustrated, distracted, and unproductive; we're certainly unable to be our most creative. In high-stress environments where perceived threats occur even more frequently, people may end up missing work altogether due to physical illness or needing a "mental health day." Under these conditions, the risk of burnout is high.

The amygdalae and limbic system, along with the brain stem, form what is commonly called the "old brain." In fact, the brain stem is sometimes referred to as the "reptilian brain" because it can be found in all vertebrates, including reptiles and mammals. It has to do with our most basic functions: breathing, sleeping, blood circulation, muscle contraction, reproduction and self-preservation. Coupled with the limbic system's early warning system of danger, the reptilian brain provides a powerful image and an important clue in how behavior manifests during distress.

"Picture the angry team leader raging in a team meeting," says Dwight Frindt. "It doesn't take a great leap from there to imagine everyone around the table instantly transformed into iguanas, geckos, and gila monsters, each caught in their own reaction and defensive/offensive posturing. It is hard to imagine that many executives actually intend to have their companies managed by a group of reptiles. Yet this kind of behavior is regularly triggered and allowed to persist."

Given the primitive, instinctual physical reactions associated with being upset, it's no wonder that all those advanced conceptual-learning approaches are not very helpful in reducing the effects of emotional distress.

The information we learn in those training workshops are accessed and processed in the cerebral cortex, the "new," rational part of the brain. But as we've seen, when we get upset we begin functioning from an entirely different place, a different part of the brain.

So how do we bridge the gap between the thinking and feeling brain? How do we make use of both our higher reasoning and our emotional passion that fires so much of our inspiration and creativity? How do we do so in a way that minimizes reactivity and distress while increasing productivity and shared pride of ownership?

Leaders can use the answers to get more of their own thoughtful time back and enhance their ability to focus on critical business issues. Team members can use the answers to raise their individual and collective productivity in ways that enhance their lives rather than increasing their stress. In both cases, people are able to move from an experience of trying to survive to one of thriving.

The Frindts propose that leaders start by working on themselves. The truth is, organizations look to their executives to set the tone. If those executives are highly reactive, in all likelihood their organizations will be, too. On the other hand, if leaders learn to identify and clear their own emotional distress first, they'll be more productive, they'll trigger less stress within their teams, and they'll be much better equipped to support team members in navigating their own emotional reactions.

Dwight and Suzanne Frindt have seen it time and again. As leaders begin to experience the benefits of their increased ability to "de-stress" emotionally, it becomes an obvious investment to train others. Just as mounting stress can create its own snowball effect in a team, team members can begin to build a new kind momentum of converting distress to eustress (healthy, productive stress—as in the excitement of pursuing a challenging goal). The more individuals there are who can identify and clear their own emotional distress, the easier it becomes for other colleagues to join them in maintaining a balance of thoughtful productivity and emotional engagement. It's a process that, when fully committed to, can transform a culture.

While lasting change takes time and continuous practice, there are a few simple, critically important steps that can begin to immediately repair the damage of emotional distress. These diagnostic and intervention steps are both conceptual and physical. They give your intellect the information and your body the tools to change both experience and behavior.

✦ 5-Step Recipe for Identifying and Clearing Distress

1. Learn to observe and identify body sensations that signal a "limbic hijacking" is taking place. It sounds obvious, but many people have no awareness of their physical state when they're upset. Yet this information is critical to implementing lasting change. So practice. With a bit of self-observation, most of us can say (for example), "I feel pressure in my chest," "I feel blood rushing to my neck," "I stiffen up," "I get this feeling in the pit of my stomach." It's essential to develop the skill of recognizing your physical symptoms. It's so important, in fact, that this physical information comes before anything else in the intervention process. Practice this step until you have a clear understanding of your reactions.

2. Exhale and slow down your breathing. After you've learned to identify that you're in a "hijacked" state, you can incorporate the practice of altering your breathing. The quickest and most effective method to immediately calm the "fight or flight" response is to take long, slow, deep breaths. When stressed, it's common to hold your breath or to take very shallow breaths as part of your defensive response. Exhaling fully and slowing down your breathing is simple. It's also quite possibly the most important and powerful antidote to emotional distress.

3. Identify your amygdalae-triggered reaction. Learn to observe your automatic defense. Are you doing fight (assertiveness/attack), flight (mentally checking out or even physically leaving the room), freeze (deer-in-the-headlights, unable to think of what to do next), or appease ("sucking up," e.g., "Oh, yes, I know exactly what you mean," or "I'm with you on that.")? Depending on the circumstances, you're likely to have one reaction that triggers as your default defensive position. As you realize what your reaction is, you'll also start to see its limits and its impact on others. This awareness actually builds the capacity to choose different behavior that gets you more of what you intend.

4. Stop trying to drive your agenda. When under emotional distress, you're more likely to make statements that you'll later wish you could eat (and may have to). One of the most productive steps you can take in a moment of upset is to stop talking, breathe, and observe. Allow yourself some time. Is there really a reason to rush? If you can learn to step back and observe your own distress, or simply stay calm in the face of another's distress, there's an opportunity for a positive outcome.

5. Ask yourself a "brain-switching" question. The amygdalae can only respond to a perceived threat, such as "Is that a bear, and is it going to eat me?" Unfortunately, since they cannot tell the difference between a physical threat and a threat in language, they go off frequently in the office or home where there hasn't been a bear sighting in years. You can reactivate your thinking capacities by coming up with a reminder question. Use this question consistently (almost like a mantra) to activate the cerebral cortex of the brain. For example, ask yourself something that brings you back to a big-picture perspective: "What is the purpose of this meeting?" "What are we committed to here?" The relative sophistication of such a question will refocus your thinking and energy and will allow your system to relax.

⚜ *One Last Thought*

NEXT COMES PRACTICE, practice, and more practice. You (and everyone else) have had decades of practice with your specific defensive reactions to distress. These reactions can be triggered by so many kinds of comments, tones of voice, and even facial expressions that you'll have to work hard to refine your "brain switching." In the beginning, it may not be possible to catch yourself before you're already in the throes of a defensive, stressful conversation. However, with practice it's possible to read the symptoms of defensiveness in your body and to mitigate the oncoming emotional reactions. If you commit yourself, it will become a lifelong discipline, and it will be well worth it.

10

⅄ Parting Thoughts

"The glory of great men should always be measured
by the means they have used to acquire it."
La Rochefoucauld

COMMUNICATION HAS COME so far over the years. In less than a split second, we can send emails to thirty different people around the world and everyone will receive the same data. Yet the most difficult challenge that can cost organizations thousands if not millions of dollars is still miscommunication in interpersonal exchanges. It's amazing that this one area has not changed in thousands of years. One could say to a group, "Think of a whale." Everyone in the room will have a different vision of a whale in their mind's eye. Similarly, the occasion for a misunderstanding can occur easily when someone is sharing an idea or giving an assignment.

A lack of loyalty and connection to an organization can develop if people feel misunderstood or not valued. This can result in turnover and the loss of top talent. We are often contacted by individuals who have graduated from top schools, have a good job history, and are looking for career guidance. When they are asked why they are looking to leave their current position, we usually hear that they do not feel valued, engaged, or appreciated. They are typically high-level performers, and the loss to their employers is costly. If organizations take time to simply manage individuals according to their needs rather than just treating them like a mechanical part, then these star performers probably would not have the need to look for other opportunities.

Each of us is a valuable part of the whole, and we need to develop an empathic company culture in order to open lines of communication for creative contribution. That leads to engagement of ideas and respect so individuals feel that they can participate in a vision. Developing a supportive environment that encourages mentoring will create opportunities for knowledge to be shared with the various generations. Additionally, this provides a creative foundation for new and exciting processes, products, and services.

⚜ *Cracking the Interpersonal Communication Code*

BUT WHERE TO begin? How do we crack the interpersonal communication code? First, include others on your team or in your department in the discussion and ask the following questions:

> ➤ What is an area of your interpersonal communication that is not working as well as you would like?

> ➤ Have you seen this come up before? Give an example.

> ➤ What would the ideal outcome look like?

> ➤ What are you doing that is not working?

> ➤ What are you doing that is working?

Next, analyze the answers and look for patterns. Now you can start to develop an action plan. Be sure to utilize information from an in-depth work style and personality assessment as described in Chapter 5 that provides the eight ways to gain true insight into personality. This knowledge will illuminate a more effective way to communicate, encourage greater engagement of individuals, and contribute to creating respect, loyalty, and appreciation. The end results: enhanced retention, performance, and positive word of mouth for attracting top talent.

Over the next 10 to 30 years, finding qualified people is going to get more difficult with a predominantly maturing population. Retention of top people will be more important than ever, and positioning your organization for recruitment purposes is vital. People talk and reputations get developed very quickly through the Internet and word of mouth. How your organization communicates within itself is a good indication of how it communicates to the outside world. Putting people in the "right" position will lead to greater job satisfaction and success.

We knew one organization that placed a very high performing accounting coordinator into a sales role. This person was very unhappy and ended up leaving the company. If they would have simply recognized the skills and desires of the individual, they would not have lost a top performer. If someone is a troubleshooter, let them troubleshoot. If someone is in need of a process then strive to provide that for them. If someone is very creative then tap into it; otherwise, they could feel unchallenged and bored. When we strive to understand people's strengths and manage accordingly, we then set them up for success. Use the information you gathered during the interview process, reference checking, and an in-depth work style and personality assessment to gain deeper insight for how to effectively work together.

⸙ *A Success Story*

ONE FINAL STORY. An organization with a customer service department was not meeting the volume level they had set for inbound calls. The manager blamed the reps and identified them as "C" players. Later, this manager was placed in a different department and a new manager was brought in. This person sat down with each individual and then with the whole group. The manager utilized information collected from in-depth work style and personality assessments of the team to understand the team members.

As a team, they discovered that within twenty-four hours of delivery, calls were coming in to inquire about the time of the delivery and additional questions about the product. The team brainstormed ideas of how to reduce the inbound questions so that they could take new order calls. Together they came up with a simple idea of providing updates to the customer regarding the delivery as well as creating an information page for the typical product/delivery questions. The call volume changed dramatically. The team members were later asked why these ideas had not been suggested in the past. The response was very simple—no one had ever asked them. They had been reprimanded for lack of performance rather then asking for their input in order to solve the problem. The results were improved productivity, performance, and job satisfaction, since they now had an environment that invited participation and teamwork.

⚜ *Action Items*

THE FOLLOWING ARE some action items to consider:

1. Contact Lighthouse Consulting Services, LLC to learn how you can use an in-depth work style and personality assessment for the hiring process, staff development, and personal growth (www.lighthouseconsulting.com).

2. Utilize the information gathered from in-depth work style and personality assessments to manage more effectively. This will in turn reduce the learning curve for on-boarding and help to better understand the individuals that you work with.

3. Place yourself and others in positions that take advantage of strengths to ensure success.

4. Be clear with expectations, listen carefully and paraphrase when something seems to be an obstacle for the person.

5. Take the time to mentor people to succeed through empathic understanding of how they might approach an opportunity or challenge, and work together to build a common bridge.

We would love to hear from you on how you have utilized the ideas shared in *Cracking the Personality Code*. Please share your thoughts with us at www.crackingthepersonalitycode.com. You can learn more about in-depth work style and personality assessments and how to incorporate them into a hiring and staff development process for your organization by visiting our website, www.lighthouseconsulting.com. There you can sign up for our *Keeping on Track* publication that provides monthly proactive articles.

/// *Books on Hiring and Managing*

General Business

Friedman, Thomas. *The World is Flat: A Brief History of the Twenty-First Century.* 2005.

Frindt, Suzanne and Dwight. *Productive Interactions.* 2008.

Gerber, Michael. *The E-Myth Revisited.* 1995.

Peters, Tom. *Reimagine!: Business Excellence in a Disruptive Age.* 2006.

Career

Bolles, Richard. *What Color Is Your Parachute? 2008: A Practical Manual for Job-Hunters and Career-Changers.* 2008.

Deutsch, Barry, and Remillard, Brad. *This is NOT the Position I Accepted: Executive Recruiters Reveal the Secrets How to Reduce Your Time in Search.* 2008. (To obtain a special discount, go to www.ImpactHiringSolutions.com and use the code, Lighthouse Consulting 5500.)

Hiring

Beutlet, Larry E., and Groth-Marnat, Gary. *Integrative Assessment of Adult Personality.* 2005.

Boydell, Janet, Deutsch, Barry, and Remillard, Brad. *You're Not the Person I Hired*. 2005. (To obtain a special discount, go to www.ImpactHiring Solutions.com and use the code, Lighthouse Consulting 5500.)

Clifford, Stephanie. "The New Science of Hiring." *Inc.* (August 2006): 93–97.

Weiss, Donald H. *Fair, Square and Legal: Safe Hiring, Managing and Firing Practices to Keep You and Your Company Out of Court*. 2004.

Management

Carter, Dr. Jay. *Nasty People*. 2003.

Brinkman, Dr. Rick and Kirschner, Dr. Rick. *Dealing with Difficult People: 24 Lessons for Bringing out the Best in Everyone*. 2003.

De Raad, B., and Perugini, M. *Big Five Assessment*. 2002.

Heller, Bruce. *The Prodigal Executive--How to Coach Executives Too Painful to Keep, Too Valuable to Fire*. 2008.

Hunter, James. *The Servant: A Simple Story about the True Essence of Leadership*. 1998.

Lencioni, Patrick. *The Five Dysfunctions of a Team*. 2002.

Piani, Judith A., Bookin-Weiner, Hedy, and Smith, Sharon. *Trait Secrets: Winning Together When You DON'T Think Alike*. 2000.

Scott, Susan. *Fierce Conversations: Achieving Success at Work and in Life One Conversation at a Time*. 2004.

Spiegelman, Paul. *Why Is Everyone Smiling? The Secret Behind Passion, Productivity, and Profit*. 2007.

Tolle, Eckhart. *The Power of Now*. 2005.

Walker, Paul David. *Unleashing Genius: Leading Yourself, Teams and Corporations*. 2008.

Wilson, Larry. *Play to Win*. 1998.

Personal Growth

Canfield, Jack. *The Success Principles: How to Get from Where You Are to Where You Want to Be*. 2005.

Carnegie, Dale. *How to Win Friends and Influence People*. 1936; *How to Stop Worrying and Start Living*. 1944

Chopra, Deepak. *The Spiritual Laws of Success*. 1994.

Covey, Stephen. *The Seven Habits of Highly Effective People*. 1990.

Frankl, Viktor. *Man's Search for Meaning*. 1946.

Hill, Napoleon. *Think and Grow Rich*. 1960.

O'Kelly, Gene. *Chasing Daylight*. 2005.

Rauchwerger, Boaz. *The Tiberias Transformation: How to Change Your Life in Less than Eight Minutes a Day*. 2001.

Schwartz, David. *The Magic of Thinking Big*. 1987.

Tolle, Eckhart. *The New Earth*. 2005.

Psychological Testing

Aiken, Lewis R. *Personality Assessment Methods and Practices*. 1999.
Aiken, Lewis R. *Personality: Theories, Assessment, Research, and Applications*. 2000.

Anastasi, Anne, and Susana Urbina. *Psychological Testing*. 1997.

Barrick, Murray R., and Michael K. Mount. "The Big Five Personality Dimensions and Job Performance: A Meta Analysis." *Personnel Psychology* 44 (1991): 1–26.

Hoffman, Edward. *Psychological Testing at Work: How to Use, Interpret, and Get the Most out of the Newest Tests in Personality, Learning Style, Aptitudes, Interests, and More*. 2001.

Hoffman, Edward. *Ace the Corporate Personality Test.* 2000.

Howard, Pierce J. *The Owner's Manual for Personality at Work.* 2000.

Kroeger, Otto. *Type Talk at Work: How the Sixteen Personality Types Determine Your Success on the Job.* 2002.

Matthews, Gerald, and Deary, Ian J. *Personality Traits.* 1998.

McCrae, Robert R., and Paul T. Costa, Jr. "Validation of the Five-Factor Model of Personality Across Instruments and Observers." *Journal of Personality and Social Psychology* 52, no. 1 (1987): 81–90.

McFarland, Lynn A., and Ann Marie Ryan. "Variance in Faking Across Non-cognitive Measures." *Journal of Applied Psychology* 85, no. 5 (2000): 812–821.

Pervin, Lawrence A. *Handbook of Personality: Theory and Research.* 1992.

Roberts, Brent W. *Personality Psychology in the Workplace.* 2001.

Schneider, Benjamin, and Smith, Brent D. *Personality and Organizations.* Mahwah, NJ: Lawrence Erlbaum Associates, 2004.

Wiggins, Jerry S. *Paradigms of Personality Assessment.* 2005.

∭ Resources from Lighthouse Consulting Services LLC

To RECEIVE RESOURCE materials on topics ranging from management and supervision to interpersonal communications:

- ➢ Subscribe to our free monthly publication, *Keeping on Track*, by going to www.lighthouseconsulting.com .
- ➢ Discussion guide is available at www.crackingthepersonalitycode.com
- ➢ Resource materials – Go to www.crackingthepersonalitycode.com

Lighthouse Consulting Services, LLC (LCS), offers business programs to help companies increase executive and employee productivity and wellbeing. These programs include in-depth work style and personality assessment testing, interpersonal coaching, and workshops on a variety of topics.

∭ In-Depth Work Style and Personality Assessments

LOOKING TO REDUCE the guesswork in your hiring decisions? Finding the best employees for your open positions can often be challenging. Excessive turnover costs your organization time, money, and lost opportunities. But with in-depth work style and personality assessment testing, you can quickly obtain objective information on a candidate's strengths and weaknesses, interview questions, and expert guidance on how best to manage that individual in your organization. Lighthouse Consulting Services can assist you in Cracking the Personality Code.

⚜ *Interpersonal Coaching*

Have you ever had a miscommunication with your employees or co-workers that resulted in costly errors or poor performance? You can avoid this by using specific communication techniques that ultimately save companies money and increase bottom-line returns. If you have an individual needing help with interpersonal skills, LCS can tailor a program to your situation. After a thorough work-style assessment, LCS provides you with an analysis, specific assignments to coach employee improvement as well as follow-up coaching sessions to monitor progress.

⚜ *Workshops and Presentations*

Looking to increase employee productivity? As with many things, communication is key. Studies show that when management uses a supportive communicational style in the workplace, employee satisfaction and productivity increases. And who can't benefit from increased productivity? Additionally, many organizations find that when employees are better skilled in effective communication, their ability to listen to instructions and communicate with coworkers and supervisors improves. Introducing your staff to these specific communication techniques through LCS workshops not only saves money, but increases the return on a valuable investment—your employees. Go to www.crackingthepersonalitycode.com for information on our workshop series.

⅏ About the Authors

Dana Borowka, MA, CEO of Lighthouse Consulting Services, LLC, has over twenty-five years of experience in business consulting. He has an undergraduate degree in human behavior and a master's degree in clinical psychology. He speaks to Vistage International and other CEO peer groups, corporations, associations and trade organizations.

Ellen Borowka, MA, COO of Lighthouse Consulting Services, LLC, has an undergraduate degree in sociology and a master's degree in counseling psychology.

Together they founded Lighthouse Consulting Services, LLC (LCS) in 1994 to provide programs to help companies increase executive and employee productivity and wellbeing. Their clients include a wide range of companies and organizations, ranging from small start-ups to Fortune 500 firms. The Borowkas are also nationally recognized as experts in their field, with regular appearances on television and radio. In addition to a weekly show that aired on KSCA 101.9FM (Los Angeles), they have also provided expert commentary for dozens of radio and news programs across the country, as well as national publications.

Index

www.crackingthepersonalitycode.com
www.lighthouseconsulting.com

Made in the USA
Lexington, KY
08 November 2010